"WINE IS BOTTLED POETRY"

ROBERT LOUIS STEVENSON

THIS JOURNAL BELONGS TO

PERFECT BOUND

WINE _____ **DATE** _____

GRAPE _____ **VINTAGE** _____
PRODUCER _____ **REGION** _____
PRICE _____ **ALCHOOL %** _____

COLOR

| RED | WHITE | ROSE' | SPARKLING | EFFERVESCENT | FORTIFIED |

APPEARANCE

| THIN | TRANSLUCENT | SATURATED | OPAQUE |

BODY

| LIGHT | LIGHT TO MED. | MEDIUM | MED. TO FULL | FULL |

SMELL

- ☐ TOAST
- ☐ TOBACCO
- ☐ LEATHER
- ☐ MUSHROOM
- ☐ JAM
- ☐ CHOCOLATE
- ☐ COFFEE
- ☐ SMOKE
- ☐ PEPPER
- ☐ MINT
- ☐ SPICE
- ☐ ALMOND
- ☐ CITRUS
- ☐ MELON
- ☐ OAK
- ☐ BERRIES
- ☐ NUTMEG
- ☐ VEGETAL
- ☐ HONEY
- ☐ APPLE
- ☐ TROPICAL
- ☐ GRASS
- ☐ FLORAL
- ☐ BUTTER
- ☐ ....
- ☐ ....
- ☐ ....
- ☐ ....
- ☐ ....
- ☐ ....

TASTE

- ☐ DARK FRUIT
- ☐ BERRIES
- ☐ PLUMS
- ☐ MUSHROOM
- ☐ TOBACCO
- ☐ CHOCOLATE
- ☐ EARTH
- ☐ PEPPER
- ☐ VANILLA
- ☐ COFFEE
- ☐ LICORICE
- ☐ LEATHER
- ☐ TOAST
- ☐ GRASS
- ☐ CITRUS
- ☐ MELON
- ☐ LYCHEE
- ☐ ALMOND
- ☐ NUTMEG
- ☐ VEGETAL
- ☐ FLORAL
- ☐ HONEY
- ☐ PEARS
- ☐ PEACHES
- ☐ ....
- ☐ ....
- ☐ ....
- ☐ ....
- ☐ ....
- ☐ ....

DRY / SWEETNESS
| 1 | 2 | 3 | 4 | 5 | 6 | 7 | 8 | 9 | 10 |

BALANCE
| 1 | 2 | 3 | 4 | 5 | 6 | 7 | 8 | 9 | 10 |

TANNINS
| 1 | 2 | 3 | 4 | 5 | 6 | 7 | 8 | 9 | 10 |

FLOVOUR INTENSITY
| 1 | 2 | 3 | 4 | 5 | 6 | 7 | 8 | 9 | 10 |

FINISH

| SHORT | SHORT TO MED. | MEDIUM | MED. TO LONG | LONG |

NOTES

PRICE TO VALUE
| 1 | 2 | 3 | 4 | 5 | 6 | 7 | 8 | 9 | 10 |

OVERALL RATING
| 1 | 2 | 3 | 4 | 5 | 6 | 7 | 8 | 9 | 10 |

WINE _____ **DATE** _____

GRAPE _____ **VINTAGE** _____
PRODUCER _____ **REGION** _____
PRICE _____ **ALCHOOL %** _____

COLOR

RED	WHITE	ROSE'	SPARKLING	EFFERVESCENT	FORTIFIED

APPEARANCE

THIN	TRANSLUCENT	SATURATED	OPAQUE

BODY

LIGHT	LIGHT TO MED.	MEDIUM	MED. TO FULL	FULL

SMELL

- ☐ TOAST
- ☐ TOBACCO
- ☐ LEATHER
- ☐ MUSHROOM
- ☐ JAM
- ☐ CHOCOLATE
- ☐ COFFEE
- ☐ SMOKE
- ☐ PEPPER
- ☐ MINT
- ☐ SPICE
- ☐ ALMOND
- ☐ CITRUS
- ☐ MELON
- ☐ OAK
- ☐ BERRIES
- ☐ NUTMEG
- ☐ VEGETAL
- ☐ HONEY
- ☐ APPLE
- ☐ TROPICAL
- ☐ GRASS
- ☐ FLORAL
- ☐ BUTTER
- ☐ ....
- ☐ ....
- ☐ ....
- ☐ ....
- ☐ ....
- ☐ ....

TASTE

- ☐ DARK FRUIT
- ☐ BERRIES
- ☐ PLUMS
- ☐ MUSHROOM
- ☐ TOBACCO
- ☐ CHOCOLATE
- ☐ EARTH
- ☐ PEPPER
- ☐ VANILLA
- ☐ COFFEE
- ☐ LICORICE
- ☐ LEATHER
- ☐ TOAST
- ☐ GRASS
- ☐ CITRUS
- ☐ MELON
- ☐ LYCHEE
- ☐ ALMOND
- ☐ NUTMEG
- ☐ VEGETAL
- ☐ FLORAL
- ☐ HONEY
- ☐ PEARS
- ☐ PEACHES
- ☐ ....
- ☐ ....
- ☐ ....
- ☐ ....
- ☐ ....
- ☐ ....

DRY / SWEETNESS
1	2	3	4	5	6	7	8	9	10

BALANCE
1	2	3	4	5	6	7	8	9	10

TANNINS
1	2	3	4	5	6	7	8	9	10

FLOVOUR INTENSITY
1	2	3	4	5	6	7	8	9	10

FINISH

SHORT	SHORT TO MED.	MEDIUM	MED. TO LONG	LONG

NOTES

_____
_____
_____
_____

PRICE TO VALUE
1	2	3	4	5	6	7	8	9	10

OVERALL RATING
1	2	3	4	5	6	7	8	9	10

WINE _____ **DATE** _____

GRAPE _____ **VINTAGE** _____
PRODUCER _____ **REGION** _____
PRICE _____ **ALCHOOL %** _____

COLOR

RED	WHITE	ROSE'	SPARKLING	EFFERVESCENT	FORTIFIED

APPEARANCE

THIN	TRANSLUCENT	SATURATED	OPAQUE

BODY

LIGHT	LIGHT TO MED.	MEDIUM	MED. TO FULL	FULL

SMELL

- ☐ TOAST
- ☐ TOBACCO
- ☐ LEATHER
- ☐ MUSHROOM
- ☐ JAM
- ☐ CHOCOLATE
- ☐ COFFEE
- ☐ SMOKE
- ☐ PEPPER
- ☐ MINT
- ☐ SPICE
- ☐ ALMOND
- ☐ CITRUS
- ☐ MELON
- ☐ OAK
- ☐ BERRIES
- ☐ NUTMEG
- ☐ VEGETAL
- ☐ HONEY
- ☐ APPLE
- ☐ TROPICAL
- ☐ GRASS
- ☐ FLORAL
- ☐ BUTTER
- ☐ ....
- ☐ ....
- ☐ ....
- ☐ ....
- ☐ ....
- ☐ ....

TASTE

- ☐ DARK FRUIT
- ☐ BERRIES
- ☐ PLUMS
- ☐ MUSHROOM
- ☐ TOBACCO
- ☐ CHOCOLATE
- ☐ EARTH
- ☐ PEPPER
- ☐ VANILLA
- ☐ COFFEE
- ☐ LICORICE
- ☐ LEATHER
- ☐ TOAST
- ☐ GRASS
- ☐ CITRUS
- ☐ MELON
- ☐ LYCHEE
- ☐ ALMOND
- ☐ NUTMEG
- ☐ VEGETAL
- ☐ FLORAL
- ☐ HONEY
- ☐ PEARS
- ☐ PEACHES
- ☐ ....
- ☐ ....
- ☐ ....
- ☐ ....
- ☐ ....
- ☐ ....

DRY / SWEETNESS

1	2	3	4	5	6	7	8	9	10

BALANCE

1	2	3	4	5	6	7	8	9	10

TANNINS

1	2	3	4	5	6	7	8	9	10

FLOVOUR INTENSITY

1	2	3	4	5	6	7	8	9	10

FINISH

SHORT	SHORT TO MED.	MEDIUM	MED. TO LONG	LONG

NOTES
_____
_____
_____
_____
_____

PRICE TO VALUE

1	2	3	4	5	6	7	8	9	10

OVERALL RATING

1	2	3	4	5	6	7	8	9	10

WINE _____   **DATE** _____

GRAPE _____   **VINTAGE** _____
PRODUCER _____   **REGION** _____
PRICE _____   **ALCHOOL %** _____

COLOR

RED	WHITE	ROSE	SPARKLING	EFFERVESCENT	FORTIFIED

APPEARANCE

THIN	TRANSLUCENT	SATURATED	OPAQUE

BODY

LIGHT	LIGHT TO MED.	MEDIUM	MED. TO FULL	FULL

SMELL

- ☐ TOAST
- ☐ TOBACCO
- ☐ LEATHER
- ☐ MUSHROOM
- ☐ JAM
- ☐ CHOCOLATE
- ☐ COFFEE
- ☐ SMOKE
- ☐ PEPPER
- ☐ MINT
- ☐ SPICE
- ☐ ALMOND
- ☐ CITRUS
- ☐ MELON
- ☐ OAK
- ☐ BERRIES
- ☐ NUTMEG
- ☐ VEGETAL
- ☐ HONEY
- ☐ APPLE
- ☐ TROPICAL
- ☐ GRASS
- ☐ FLORAL
- ☐ BUTTER
- ☐ ....
- ☐ ....
- ☐ ....
- ☐ ....
- ☐ ....
- ☐ ....

TASTE

- ☐ DARK FRUIT
- ☐ BERRIES
- ☐ PLUMS
- ☐ MUSHROOM
- ☐ TOBACCO
- ☐ CHOCOLATE
- ☐ EARTH
- ☐ PEPPER
- ☐ VANILLA
- ☐ COFFEE
- ☐ LICORICE
- ☐ LEATHER
- ☐ TOAST
- ☐ GRASS
- ☐ CITRUS
- ☐ MELON
- ☐ LYCHEE
- ☐ ALMOND
- ☐ NUTMEG
- ☐ VEGETAL
- ☐ FLORAL
- ☐ HONEY
- ☐ PEARS
- ☐ PEACHES
- ☐ ....
- ☐ ....
- ☐ ....
- ☐ ....
- ☐ ....
- ☐ ....

DRY / SWEETNESS

1	2	3	4	5	6	7	8	9	10

BALANCE

1	2	3	4	5	6	7	8	9	10

TANNINS

1	2	3	4	5	6	7	8	9	10

FLOVOUR INTENSITY

1	2	3	4	5	6	7	8	9	10

FINISH

SHORT	SHORT TO MED.	MEDIUM	MED. TO LONG	LONG

NOTES

PRICE TO VALUE

1	2	3	4	5	6	7	8	9	10

OVERALL RATING

1	2	3	4	5	6	7	8	9	10

WINE	DATE
GRAPE	VINTAGE
PRODUCER	REGION
PRICE	ALCHOOL %

COLOR

RED	WHITE	ROSE'	SPARKLING	EFFERVESCENT	FORTIFIED

APPEARANCE

THIN	TRANSLUCENT	SATURATED	OPAQUE

BODY

LIGHT	LIGHT TO MED.	MEDIUM	MED. TO FULL	FULL

SMELL

- ☐ TOAST
- ☐ TOBACCO
- ☐ LEATHER
- ☐ MUSHROOM
- ☐ JAM
- ☐ CHOCOLATE
- ☐ COFFEE
- ☐ SMOKE
- ☐ PEPPER
- ☐ MINT
- ☐ SPICE
- ☐ ALMOND
- ☐ CITRUS
- ☐ MELON
- ☐ OAK
- ☐ BERRIES
- ☐ NUTMEG
- ☐ VEGETAL
- ☐ HONEY
- ☐ APPLE
- ☐ TROPICAL
- ☐ GRASS
- ☐ FLORAL
- ☐ BUTTER
- ☐ ....
- ☐ ....
- ☐ ....
- ☐ ....
- ☐ ....
- ☐ ....

TASTE

- ☐ DARK FRUIT
- ☐ BERRIES
- ☐ PLUMS
- ☐ MUSHROOM
- ☐ TOBACCO
- ☐ CHOCOLATE
- ☐ EARTH
- ☐ PEPPER
- ☐ VANILLA
- ☐ COFFEE
- ☐ LICORICE
- ☐ LEATHER
- ☐ TOAST
- ☐ GRASS
- ☐ CITRUS
- ☐ MELON
- ☐ LYCHEE
- ☐ ALMOND
- ☐ NUTMEG
- ☐ VEGETAL
- ☐ FLORAL
- ☐ HONEY
- ☐ PEARS
- ☐ PEACHES
- ☐ ....
- ☐ ....
- ☐ ....
- ☐ ....
- ☐ ....
- ☐ ....

DRY / SWEETNESS
1	2	3	4	5	6	7	8	9	10

BALANCE
1	2	3	4	5	6	7	8	9	10

TANNINS
1	2	3	4	5	6	7	8	9	10

FLOVOUR INTENSITY
1	2	3	4	5	6	7	8	9	10

FINISH

SHORT	SHORT TO MED.	MEDIUM	MED. TO LONG	LONG

NOTES

PRICE TO VALUE
1	2	3	4	5	6	7	8	9	10

OVERALL RATING
1	2	3	4	5	6	7	8	9	10

WINE		DATE	
GRAPE		VINTAGE	
PRODUCER		REGION	
PRICE		ALCHOOL %	

COLOR

RED	WHITE	ROSE'	SPARKLING	EFFERVESCENT	FORTIFIED

APPEARANCE

THIN	TRANSLUCENT	SATURATED	OPAQUE

BODY

LIGHT	LIGHT TO MED.	MEDIUM	MED. TO FULL	FULL

SMELL

☐ TOAST	☐ COFFEE	☐ CITRUS	☐ HONEY	☐ ....
☐ TOBACCO	☐ SMOKE	☐ MELON	☐ APPLE	☐ ....
☐ LEATHER	☐ PEPPER	☐ OAK	☐ TROPICAL	☐ ....
☐ MUSHROOM	☐ MINT	☐ BERRIES	☐ GRASS	☐ ....
☐ JAM	☐ SPICE	☐ NUTMEG	☐ FLORAL	☐ ....
☐ CHOCOLATE	☐ ALMOND	☐ VEGETAL	☐ BUTTER	☐ ....

TASTE

☐ DARK FRUIT	☐ EARTH	☐ TOAST	☐ NUTMEG	☐ ....
☐ BERRIES	☐ PEPPER	☐ GRASS	☐ VEGETAL	☐ ....
☐ PLUMS	☐ VANILLA	☐ CITRUS	☐ FLORAL	☐ ....
☐ MUSHROOM	☐ COFFEE	☐ MELON	☐ HONEY	☐ ....
☐ TOBACCO	☐ LICORICE	☐ LYCHEE	☐ PEARS	☐ ....
☐ CHOCOLATE	☐ LEATHER	☐ ALMOND	☐ PEACHES	☐ ....

DRY / SWEETNESS
1	2	3	4	5	6	7	8	9	10

BALANCE
1	2	3	4	5	6	7	8	9	10

TANNINS
1	2	3	4	5	6	7	8	9	10

FLOVOUR INTENSITY
1	2	3	4	5	6	7	8	9	10

FINISH

SHORT	SHORT TO MED.	MEDIUM	MED. TO LONG	LONG

NOTES

PRICE TO VALUE
1	2	3	4	5	6	7	8	9	10

OVERALL RATING
1	2	3	4	5	6	7	8	9	10

WINE _____ **DATE** _____

GRAPE _____ **VINTAGE** _____
PRODUCER _____ **REGION** _____
PRICE _____ **ALCHOOL %** _____

COLOR

| RED | WHITE | ROSE' | SPARKLING | EFFERVESCENT | FORTIFIED |

APPEARANCE

| THIN | TRANSLUCENT | SATURATED | OPAQUE |

BODY

| LIGHT | LIGHT TO MED. | MEDIUM | MED. TO FULL | FULL |

SMELL

- ☐ TOAST
- ☐ TOBACCO
- ☐ LEATHER
- ☐ MUSHROOM
- ☐ JAM
- ☐ CHOCOLATE
- ☐ COFFEE
- ☐ SMOKE
- ☐ PEPPER
- ☐ MINT
- ☐ SPICE
- ☐ ALMOND
- ☐ CITRUS
- ☐ MELON
- ☐ OAK
- ☐ BERRIES
- ☐ NUTMEG
- ☐ VEGETAL
- ☐ HONEY
- ☐ APPLE
- ☐ TROPICAL
- ☐ GRASS
- ☐ FLORAL
- ☐ BUTTER
- ☐ ....
- ☐ ....
- ☐ ....
- ☐ ....
- ☐ ....
- ☐ ....

TASTE

- ☐ DARK FRUIT
- ☐ BERRIES
- ☐ PLUMS
- ☐ MUSHROOM
- ☐ TOBACCO
- ☐ CHOCOLATE
- ☐ EARTH
- ☐ PEPPER
- ☐ VANILLA
- ☐ COFFEE
- ☐ LICORICE
- ☐ LEATHER
- ☐ TOAST
- ☐ GRASS
- ☐ CITRUS
- ☐ MELON
- ☐ LYCHEE
- ☐ ALMOND
- ☐ NUTMEG
- ☐ VEGETAL
- ☐ FLORAL
- ☐ HONEY
- ☐ PEARS
- ☐ PEACHES
- ☐ ....
- ☐ ....
- ☐ ....
- ☐ ....
- ☐ ....
- ☐ ....

DRY / SWEETNESS
| 1 | 2 | 3 | 4 | 5 | 6 | 7 | 8 | 9 | 10 |

BALANCE
| 1 | 2 | 3 | 4 | 5 | 6 | 7 | 8 | 9 | 10 |

TANNINS
| 1 | 2 | 3 | 4 | 5 | 6 | 7 | 8 | 9 | 10 |

FLOVOUR INTENSITY
| 1 | 2 | 3 | 4 | 5 | 6 | 7 | 8 | 9 | 10 |

FINISH

| SHORT | SHORT TO MED. | MEDIUM | MED. TO LONG | LONG |

NOTES

PRICE TO VALUE
| 1 | 2 | 3 | 4 | 5 | 6 | 7 | 8 | 9 | 10 |

OVERALL RATING
| 1 | 2 | 3 | 4 | 5 | 6 | 7 | 8 | 9 | 10 |

WINE	**DATE**
GRAPE	**VINTAGE**
PRODUCER	**REGION**
PRICE	**ALCHOOL %**

COLOR

RED	WHITE	ROSE	SPARKLING	EFFERVESCENT	FORTIFIED

APPEARANCE

THIN	TRANSLUCENT	SATURATED	OPAQUE

BODY

LIGHT	LIGHT TO MED.	MEDIUM	MED. TO FULL	FULL

SMELL

- ☐ TOAST
- ☐ TOBACCO
- ☐ LEATHER
- ☐ MUSHROOM
- ☐ JAM
- ☐ CHOCOLATE
- ☐ COFFEE
- ☐ SMOKE
- ☐ PEPPER
- ☐ MINT
- ☐ SPICE
- ☐ ALMOND
- ☐ CITRUS
- ☐ MELON
- ☐ OAK
- ☐ BERRIES
- ☐ NUTMEG
- ☐ VEGETAL
- ☐ HONEY
- ☐ APPLE
- ☐ TROPICAL
- ☐ GRASS
- ☐ FLORAL
- ☐ BUTTER
- ☐ ....
- ☐ ....
- ☐ ....
- ☐ ....
- ☐ ....
- ☐ ....

TASTE

- ☐ DARK FRUIT
- ☐ BERRIES
- ☐ PLUMS
- ☐ MUSHROOM
- ☐ TOBACCO
- ☐ CHOCOLATE
- ☐ EARTH
- ☐ PEPPER
- ☐ VANILLA
- ☐ COFFEE
- ☐ LICORICE
- ☐ LEATHER
- ☐ TOAST
- ☐ GRASS
- ☐ CITRUS
- ☐ MELON
- ☐ LYCHEE
- ☐ ALMOND
- ☐ NUTMEG
- ☐ VEGETAL
- ☐ FLORAL
- ☐ HONEY
- ☐ PEARS
- ☐ PEACHES
- ☐ ....
- ☐ ....
- ☐ ....
- ☐ ....
- ☐ ....
- ☐ ....

DRY / SWEETNESS

1	2	3	4	5	6	7	8	9	10

BALANCE

1	2	3	4	5	6	7	8	9	10

TANNINS

1	2	3	4	5	6	7	8	9	10

FLOVOUR INTENSITY

1	2	3	4	5	6	7	8	9	10

FINISH

SHORT	SHORT TO MED.	MEDIUM	MED. TO LONG	LONG

NOTES

PRICE TO VALUE

1	2	3	4	5	6	7	8	9	10

OVERALL RATING

1	2	3	4	5	6	7	8	9	10

WINE   **DATE**

GRAPE   **VINTAGE**
PRODUCER   **REGION**
PRICE   **ALCHOOL %**

COLOR

RED	WHITE	ROSE	SPARKLING	EFFERVESCENT	FORTIFIED

APPEARANCE

THIN	TRANSLUCENT	SATURATED	OPAQUE

BODY

LIGHT	LIGHT TO MED.	MEDIUM	MED. TO FULL	FULL

SMELL

☐ TOAST	☐ COFFEE	☐ CITRUS	☐ HONEY	☐ ....
☐ TOBACCO	☐ SMOKE	☐ MELON	☐ APPLE	☐ ....
☐ LEATHER	☐ PEPPER	☐ OAK	☐ TROPICAL	☐ ....
☐ MUSHROOM	☐ MINT	☐ BERRIES	☐ GRASS	☐ ....
☐ JAM	☐ SPICE	☐ NUTMEG	☐ FLORAL	☐ ....
☐ CHOCOLATE	☐ ALMOND	☐ VEGETAL	☐ BUTTER	☐ ....

TASTE

☐ DARK FRUIT	☐ EARTH	☐ TOAST	☐ NUTMEG	☐ ....
☐ BERRIES	☐ PEPPER	☐ GRASS	☐ VEGETAL	☐ ....
☐ PLUMS	☐ VANILLA	☐ CITRUS	☐ FLORAL	☐ ....
☐ MUSHROOM	☐ COFFEE	☐ MELON	☐ HONEY	☐ ....
☐ TOBACCO	☐ LICORICE	☐ LYCHEE	☐ PEARS	☐ ....
☐ CHOCOLATE	☐ LEATHER	☐ ALMOND	☐ PEACHES	☐ ....

DRY / SWEETNESS
1	2	3	4	5	6	7	8	9	10

BALANCE
1	2	3	4	5	6	7	8	9	10

TANNINS
1	2	3	4	5	6	7	8	9	10

FLOVOUR INTENSITY
1	2	3	4	5	6	7	8	9	10

FINISH

SHORT	SHORT TO MED.	MEDIUM	MED. TO LONG	LONG

NOTES

PRICE TO VALUE
1	2	3	4	5	6	7	8	9	10

OVERALL RATING
1	2	3	4	5	6	7	8	9	10

WINE _____ **DATE** _____

GRAPE _____ **VINTAGE** _____
PRODUCER _____ **REGION** _____
PRICE _____ **ALCHOOL %** _____

COLOR

RED	WHITE	ROSE'	SPARKLING	EFFERVESCENT	FORTIFIED

APPEARANCE

THIN	TRANSLUCENT	SATURATED	OPAQUE

BODY

LIGHT	LIGHT TO MED.	MEDIUM	MED. TO FULL	FULL

SMELL

- ☐ TOAST
- ☐ TOBACCO
- ☐ LEATHER
- ☐ MUSHROOM
- ☐ JAM
- ☐ CHOCOLATE
- ☐ COFFEE
- ☐ SMOKE
- ☐ PEPPER
- ☐ MINT
- ☐ SPICE
- ☐ ALMOND
- ☐ CITRUS
- ☐ MELON
- ☐ OAK
- ☐ BERRIES
- ☐ NUTMEG
- ☐ VEGETAL
- ☐ HONEY
- ☐ APPLE
- ☐ TROPICAL
- ☐ GRASS
- ☐ FLORAL
- ☐ BUTTER
- ☐ ....
- ☐ ....
- ☐ ....
- ☐ ....
- ☐ ....
- ☐ ....

TASTE

- ☐ DARK FRUIT
- ☐ BERRIES
- ☐ PLUMS
- ☐ MUSHROOM
- ☐ TOBACCO
- ☐ CHOCOLATE
- ☐ EARTH
- ☐ PEPPER
- ☐ VANILLA
- ☐ COFFEE
- ☐ LICORICE
- ☐ LEATHER
- ☐ TOAST
- ☐ GRASS
- ☐ CITRUS
- ☐ MELON
- ☐ LYCHEE
- ☐ ALMOND
- ☐ NUTMEG
- ☐ VEGETAL
- ☐ FLORAL
- ☐ HONEY
- ☐ PEARS
- ☐ PEACHES
- ☐ ....
- ☐ ....
- ☐ ....
- ☐ ....
- ☐ ....
- ☐ ....

DRY / SWEETNESS

1	2	3	4	5	6	7	8	9	10

BALANCE

1	2	3	4	5	6	7	8	9	10

TANNINS

1	2	3	4	5	6	7	8	9	10

FLOVOUR INTENSITY

1	2	3	4	5	6	7	8	9	10

FINISH

SHORT	SHORT TO MED.	MEDIUM	MED. TO LONG	LONG

NOTES

_____
_____
_____
_____
_____

PRICE TO VALUE

1	2	3	4	5	6	7	8	9	10

OVERALL RATING

1	2	3	4	5	6	7	8	9	10

WINE	DATE
GRAPE	VINTAGE
PRODUCER	REGION
PRICE	ALCHOOL %

COLOR

RED	WHITE	ROSE	SPARKLING	EFFERVESCENT	FORTIFIED

APPEARANCE

THIN	TRANSLUCENT	SATURATED	OPAQUE

BODY

LIGHT	LIGHT TO MED.	MEDIUM	MED. TO FULL	FULL

SMELL

- ☐ TOAST
- ☐ TOBACCO
- ☐ LEATHER
- ☐ MUSHROOM
- ☐ JAM
- ☐ CHOCOLATE
- ☐ COFFEE
- ☐ SMOKE
- ☐ PEPPER
- ☐ MINT
- ☐ SPICE
- ☐ ALMOND
- ☐ CITRUS
- ☐ MELON
- ☐ OAK
- ☐ BERRIES
- ☐ NUTMEG
- ☐ VEGETAL
- ☐ HONEY
- ☐ APPLE
- ☐ TROPICAL
- ☐ GRASS
- ☐ FLORAL
- ☐ BUTTER
- ☐ ....
- ☐ ....
- ☐ ....
- ☐ ....
- ☐ ....
- ☐ ....

TASTE

- ☐ DARK FRUIT
- ☐ BERRIES
- ☐ PLUMS
- ☐ MUSHROOM
- ☐ TOBACCO
- ☐ CHOCOLATE
- ☐ EARTH
- ☐ PEPPER
- ☐ VANILLA
- ☐ COFFEE
- ☐ LICORICE
- ☐ LEATHER
- ☐ TOAST
- ☐ GRASS
- ☐ CITRUS
- ☐ MELON
- ☐ LYCHEE
- ☐ ALMOND
- ☐ NUTMEG
- ☐ VEGETAL
- ☐ FLORAL
- ☐ HONEY
- ☐ PEARS
- ☐ PEACHES
- ☐ ....
- ☐ ....
- ☐ ....
- ☐ ....
- ☐ ....
- ☐ ....

DRY / SWEETNESS
1	2	3	4	5	6	7	8	9	10

BALANCE
1	2	3	4	5	6	7	8	9	10

TANNINS
1	2	3	4	5	6	7	8	9	10

FLOVOUR INTENSITY
1	2	3	4	5	6	7	8	9	10

FINISH

SHORT	SHORT TO MED.	MEDIUM	MED. TO LONG	LONG

NOTES

PRICE TO VALUE
1	2	3	4	5	6	7	8	9	10

OVERALL RATING
1	2	3	4	5	6	7	8	9	10

WINE _____ **DATE** _____

GRAPE _____ **VINTAGE** _____
PRODUCER _____ **REGION** _____
PRICE _____ **ALCHOOL %** _____

COLOR

| RED | WHITE | ROSE | SPARKLING | EFFERVESCENT | FORTIFIED |

APPEARANCE

| THIN | TRANSLUCENT | SATURATED | OPAQUE |

BODY

| LIGHT | LIGHT TO MED. | MEDIUM | MED. TO FULL | FULL |

SMELL

- ☐ TOAST
- ☐ TOBACCO
- ☐ LEATHER
- ☐ MUSHROOM
- ☐ JAM
- ☐ CHOCOLATE
- ☐ COFFEE
- ☐ SMOKE
- ☐ PEPPER
- ☐ MINT
- ☐ SPICE
- ☐ ALMOND
- ☐ CITRUS
- ☐ MELON
- ☐ OAK
- ☐ BERRIES
- ☐ NUTMEG
- ☐ VEGETAL
- ☐ HONEY
- ☐ APPLE
- ☐ TROPICAL
- ☐ GRASS
- ☐ FLORAL
- ☐ BUTTER
- ☐ ....
- ☐ ....
- ☐ ....
- ☐ ....
- ☐ ....
- ☐ ....

TASTE

- ☐ DARK FRUIT
- ☐ BERRIES
- ☐ PLUMS
- ☐ MUSHROOM
- ☐ TOBACCO
- ☐ CHOCOLATE
- ☐ EARTH
- ☐ PEPPER
- ☐ VANILLA
- ☐ COFFEE
- ☐ LICORICE
- ☐ LEATHER
- ☐ TOAST
- ☐ GRASS
- ☐ CITRUS
- ☐ MELON
- ☐ LYCHEE
- ☐ ALMOND
- ☐ NUTMEG
- ☐ VEGETAL
- ☐ FLORAL
- ☐ HONEY
- ☐ PEARS
- ☐ PEACHES
- ☐ ....
- ☐ ....
- ☐ ....
- ☐ ....
- ☐ ....
- ☐ ....

DRY / SWEETNESS

| 1 | 2 | 3 | 4 | 5 | 6 | 7 | 8 | 9 | 10 |

BALANCE

| 1 | 2 | 3 | 4 | 5 | 6 | 7 | 8 | 9 | 10 |

TANNINS

| 1 | 2 | 3 | 4 | 5 | 6 | 7 | 8 | 9 | 10 |

FLOVOUR INTENSITY

| 1 | 2 | 3 | 4 | 5 | 6 | 7 | 8 | 9 | 10 |

FINISH

| SHORT | SHORT TO MED. | MEDIUM | MED. TO LONG | LONG |

NOTES

_____
_____
_____
_____
_____

PRICE TO VALUE

| 1 | 2 | 3 | 4 | 5 | 6 | 7 | 8 | 9 | 10 |

OVERALL RATING

| 1 | 2 | 3 | 4 | 5 | 6 | 7 | 8 | 9 | 10 |

WINE	DATE
GRAPE	VINTAGE
PRODUCER	REGION
PRICE	ALCHOOL %

COLOR

RED	WHITE	ROSE	SPARKLING	EFFERVESCENT	FORTIFIED

APPEARANCE

THIN	TRANSLUCENT	SATURATED	OPAQUE

BODY

LIGHT	LIGHT TO MED.	MEDIUM	MED. TO FULL	FULL

SMELL

- ☐ TOAST
- ☐ TOBACCO
- ☐ LEATHER
- ☐ MUSHROOM
- ☐ JAM
- ☐ CHOCOLATE
- ☐ COFFEE
- ☐ SMOKE
- ☐ PEPPER
- ☐ MINT
- ☐ SPICE
- ☐ ALMOND
- ☐ CITRUS
- ☐ MELON
- ☐ OAK
- ☐ BERRIES
- ☐ NUTMEG
- ☐ VEGETAL
- ☐ HONEY
- ☐ APPLE
- ☐ TROPICAL
- ☐ GRASS
- ☐ FLORAL
- ☐ BUTTER
- ☐ ....
- ☐ ....
- ☐ ....
- ☐ ....
- ☐ ....
- ☐ ....

TASTE

- ☐ DARK FRUIT
- ☐ BERRIES
- ☐ PLUMS
- ☐ MUSHROOM
- ☐ TOBACCO
- ☐ CHOCOLATE
- ☐ EARTH
- ☐ PEPPER
- ☐ VANILLA
- ☐ COFFEE
- ☐ LICORICE
- ☐ LEATHER
- ☐ TOAST
- ☐ GRASS
- ☐ CITRUS
- ☐ MELON
- ☐ LYCHEE
- ☐ ALMOND
- ☐ NUTMEG
- ☐ VEGETAL
- ☐ FLORAL
- ☐ HONEY
- ☐ PEARS
- ☐ PEACHES
- ☐ ....
- ☐ ....
- ☐ ....
- ☐ ....
- ☐ ....
- ☐ ....

DRY / SWEETNESS
1	2	3	4	5	6	7	8	9	10

BALANCE
1	2	3	4	5	6	7	8	9	10

TANNINS
1	2	3	4	5	6	7	8	9	10

FLOVOUR INTENSITY
1	2	3	4	5	6	7	8	9	10

FINISH

SHORT	SHORT TO MED.	MEDIUM	MED. TO LONG	LONG

NOTES

PRICE TO VALUE
1	2	3	4	5	6	7	8	9	10

OVERALL RATING
1	2	3	4	5	6	7	8	9	10

WINE _____ **DATE** _____

GRAPE _____ **VINTAGE** _____
PRODUCER _____ **REGION** _____
PRICE _____ **ALCHOOL %** _____

COLOR

RED	WHITE	ROSE'	SPARKLING	EFFERVESCENT	FORTIFIED

APPEARANCE

THIN	TRANSLUCENT	SATURATED	OPAQUE

BODY

LIGHT	LIGHT TO MED.	MEDIUM	MED. TO FULL	FULL

SMELL

- ☐ TOAST
- ☐ TOBACCO
- ☐ LEATHER
- ☐ MUSHROOM
- ☐ JAM
- ☐ CHOCOLATE
- ☐ COFFEE
- ☐ SMOKE
- ☐ PEPPER
- ☐ MINT
- ☐ SPICE
- ☐ ALMOND
- ☐ CITRUS
- ☐ MELON
- ☐ OAK
- ☐ BERRIES
- ☐ NUTMEG
- ☐ VEGETAL
- ☐ HONEY
- ☐ APPLE
- ☐ TROPICAL
- ☐ GRASS
- ☐ FLORAL
- ☐ BUTTER
- ☐ ....
- ☐ ....
- ☐ ....
- ☐ ....
- ☐ ....
- ☐ ....

TASTE

- ☐ DARK FRUIT
- ☐ BERRIES
- ☐ PLUMS
- ☐ MUSHROOM
- ☐ TOBACCO
- ☐ CHOCOLATE
- ☐ EARTH
- ☐ PEPPER
- ☐ VANILLA
- ☐ COFFEE
- ☐ LICORICE
- ☐ LEATHER
- ☐ TOAST
- ☐ GRASS
- ☐ CITRUS
- ☐ MELON
- ☐ LYCHEE
- ☐ ALMOND
- ☐ NUTMEG
- ☐ VEGETAL
- ☐ FLORAL
- ☐ HONEY
- ☐ PEARS
- ☐ PEACHES
- ☐ ....
- ☐ ....
- ☐ ....
- ☐ ....
- ☐ ....
- ☐ ....

DRY / SWEETNESS
1	2	3	4	5	6	7	8	9	10

BALANCE
1	2	3	4	5	6	7	8	9	10

TANNINS
1	2	3	4	5	6	7	8	9	10

FLOVOUR INTENSITY
1	2	3	4	5	6	7	8	9	10

FINISH

SHORT	SHORT TO MED.	MEDIUM	MED. TO LONG	LONG

NOTES

_____
_____
_____
_____
_____

PRICE TO VALUE
1	2	3	4	5	6	7	8	9	10

OVERALL RATING
1	2	3	4	5	6	7	8	9	10

WINE		DATE	
GRAPE		**VINTAGE**	
PRODUCER		**REGION**	
PRICE		**ALCHOOL %**	

COLOR

RED	WHITE	ROSE	SPARKLING	EFFERVESCENT	FORTIFIED

APPEARANCE

THIN	TRANSLUCENT	SATURATED	OPAQUE

BODY

LIGHT	LIGHT TO MED.	MEDIUM	MED. TO FULL	FULL

SMELL

☐ TOAST	☐ COFFEE	☐ CITRUS	☐ HONEY	☐ ....
☐ TOBACCO	☐ SMOKE	☐ MELON	☐ APPLE	☐ ....
☐ LEATHER	☐ PEPPER	☐ OAK	☐ TROPICAL	☐ ....
☐ MUSHROOM	☐ MINT	☐ BERRIES	☐ GRASS	☐ ....
☐ JAM	☐ SPICE	☐ NUTMEG	☐ FLORAL	☐ ....
☐ CHOCOLATE	☐ ALMOND	☐ VEGETAL	☐ BUTTER	☐ ....

TASTE

☐ DARK FRUIT	☐ EARTH	☐ TOAST	☐ NUTMEG	☐ ....
☐ BERRIES	☐ PEPPER	☐ GRASS	☐ VEGETAL	☐ ....
☐ PLUMS	☐ VANILLA	☐ CITRUS	☐ FLORAL	☐ ....
☐ MUSHROOM	☐ COFFEE	☐ MELON	☐ HONEY	☐ ....
☐ TOBACCO	☐ LICORICE	☐ LYCHEE	☐ PEARS	☐ ....
☐ CHOCOLATE	☐ LEATHER	☐ ALMOND	☐ PEACHES	☐ ....

DRY / SWEETNESS

1	2	3	4	5	6	7	8	9	10

BALANCE

1	2	3	4	5	6	7	8	9	10

TANNINS

1	2	3	4	5	6	7	8	9	10

FLOVOUR INTENSITY

1	2	3	4	5	6	7	8	9	10

FINISH

SHORT	SHORT TO MED.	MEDIUM	MED. TO LONG	LONG

NOTES

PRICE TO VALUE

1	2	3	4	5	6	7	8	9	10

OVERALL RATING

1	2	3	4	5	6	7	8	9	10

WINE		DATE	
GRAPE		VINTAGE	
PRODUCER		REGION	
PRICE		ALCHOOL %	

COLOR

RED	WHITE	ROSE	SPARKLING	EFFERVESCENT	FORTIFIED

APPEARANCE

THIN	TRANSLUCENT	SATURATED	OPAQUE

BODY

LIGHT	LIGHT TO MED.	MEDIUM	MED. TO FULL	FULL

SMELL

- ☐ TOAST
- ☐ TOBACCO
- ☐ LEATHER
- ☐ MUSHROOM
- ☐ JAM
- ☐ CHOCOLATE
- ☐ COFFEE
- ☐ SMOKE
- ☐ PEPPER
- ☐ MINT
- ☐ SPICE
- ☐ ALMOND
- ☐ CITRUS
- ☐ MELON
- ☐ OAK
- ☐ BERRIES
- ☐ NUTMEG
- ☐ VEGETAL
- ☐ HONEY
- ☐ APPLE
- ☐ TROPICAL
- ☐ GRASS
- ☐ FLORAL
- ☐ BUTTER
- ☐ ....
- ☐ ....
- ☐ ....
- ☐ ....
- ☐ ....
- ☐ ....

TASTE

- ☐ DARK FRUIT
- ☐ BERRIES
- ☐ PLUMS
- ☐ MUSHROOM
- ☐ TOBACCO
- ☐ CHOCOLATE
- ☐ EARTH
- ☐ PEPPER
- ☐ VANILLA
- ☐ COFFEE
- ☐ LICORICE
- ☐ LEATHER
- ☐ TOAST
- ☐ GRASS
- ☐ CITRUS
- ☐ MELON
- ☐ LYCHEE
- ☐ ALMOND
- ☐ NUTMEG
- ☐ VEGETAL
- ☐ FLORAL
- ☐ HONEY
- ☐ PEARS
- ☐ PEACHES
- ☐ ....
- ☐ ....
- ☐ ....
- ☐ ....
- ☐ ....
- ☐ ....

DRY / SWEETNESS

1	2	3	4	5	6	7	8	9	10

BALANCE

1	2	3	4	5	6	7	8	9	10

TANNINS

1	2	3	4	5	6	7	8	9	10

FLOVOUR INTENSITY

1	2	3	4	5	6	7	8	9	10

FINISH

SHORT	SHORT TO MED.	MEDIUM	MED. TO LONG	LONG

NOTES

PRICE TO VALUE

1	2	3	4	5	6	7	8	9	10

OVERALL RATING

1	2	3	4	5	6	7	8	9	10

WINE		DATE	
GRAPE		VINTAGE	
PRODUCER		REGION	
PRICE		ALCHOOL %	

COLOR

RED	WHITE	ROSE'	SPARKLING	EFFERVESCENT	FORTIFIED

APPEARANCE

THIN	TRANSLUCENT	SATURATED	OPAQUE

BODY

LIGHT	LIGHT TO MED.	MEDIUM	MED. TO FULL	FULL

SMELL

☐ TOAST	☐ COFFEE	☐ CITRUS	☐ HONEY	☐ ....
☐ TOBACCO	☐ SMOKE	☐ MELON	☐ APPLE	☐ ....
☐ LEATHER	☐ PEPPER	☐ OAK	☐ TROPICAL	☐ ....
☐ MUSHROOM	☐ MINT	☐ BERRIES	☐ GRASS	☐ ....
☐ JAM	☐ SPICE	☐ NUTMEG	☐ FLORAL	☐ ....
☐ CHOCOLATE	☐ ALMOND	☐ VEGETAL	☐ BUTTER	☐ ....

TASTE

☐ DARK FRUIT	☐ EARTH	☐ TOAST	☐ NUTMEG	☐ ....
☐ BERRIES	☐ PEPPER	☐ GRASS	☐ VEGETAL	☐ ....
☐ PLUMS	☐ VANILLA	☐ CITRUS	☐ FLORAL	☐ ....
☐ MUSHROOM	☐ COFFEE	☐ MELON	☐ HONEY	☐ ....
☐ TOBACCO	☐ LICORICE	☐ LYCHEE	☐ PEARS	☐ ....
☐ CHOCOLATE	☐ LEATHER	☐ ALMOND	☐ PEACHES	☐ ....

DRY / SWEETNESS

1	2	3	4	5	6	7	8	9	10

BALANCE

1	2	3	4	5	6	7	8	9	10

TANNINS

1	2	3	4	5	6	7	8	9	10

FLOVOUR INTENSITY

1	2	3	4	5	6	7	8	9	10

FINISH

SHORT	SHORT TO MED.	MEDIUM	MED. TO LONG	LONG

NOTES

PRICE TO VALUE

1	2	3	4	5	6	7	8	9	10

OVERALL RATING

1	2	3	4	5	6	7	8	9	10

WINE _____ **DATE** _____

GRAPE _____ **VINTAGE** _____
PRODUCER _____ **REGION** _____
PRICE _____ **ALCHOOL %** _____

COLOR

| RED | WHITE | ROSE' | SPARKLING | EFFERVESCENT | FORTIFIED |

APPEARANCE

| THIN | TRANSLUCENT | SATURATED | OPAQUE |

BODY

| LIGHT | LIGHT TO MED. | MEDIUM | MED. TO FULL | FULL |

SMELL

- ☐ TOAST
- ☐ TOBACCO
- ☐ LEATHER
- ☐ MUSHROOM
- ☐ JAM
- ☐ CHOCOLATE
- ☐ COFFEE
- ☐ SMOKE
- ☐ PEPPER
- ☐ MINT
- ☐ SPICE
- ☐ ALMOND
- ☐ CITRUS
- ☐ MELON
- ☐ OAK
- ☐ BERRIES
- ☐ NUTMEG
- ☐ VEGETAL
- ☐ HONEY
- ☐ APPLE
- ☐ TROPICAL
- ☐ GRASS
- ☐ FLORAL
- ☐ BUTTER
- ☐ ....
- ☐ ....
- ☐ ....
- ☐ ....
- ☐ ....
- ☐ ....

TASTE

- ☐ DARK FRUIT
- ☐ BERRIES
- ☐ PLUMS
- ☐ MUSHROOM
- ☐ TOBACCO
- ☐ CHOCOLATE
- ☐ EARTH
- ☐ PEPPER
- ☐ VANILLA
- ☐ COFFEE
- ☐ LICORICE
- ☐ LEATHER
- ☐ TOAST
- ☐ GRASS
- ☐ CITRUS
- ☐ MELON
- ☐ LYCHEE
- ☐ ALMOND
- ☐ NUTMEG
- ☐ VEGETAL
- ☐ FLORAL
- ☐ HONEY
- ☐ PEARS
- ☐ PEACHES
- ☐ ....
- ☐ ....
- ☐ ....
- ☐ ....
- ☐ ....
- ☐ ....

DRY / SWEETNESS
| 1 | 2 | 3 | 4 | 5 | 6 | 7 | 8 | 9 | 10 |

BALANCE
| 1 | 2 | 3 | 4 | 5 | 6 | 7 | 8 | 9 | 10 |

TANNINS
| 1 | 2 | 3 | 4 | 5 | 6 | 7 | 8 | 9 | 10 |

FLOVOUR INTENSITY
| 1 | 2 | 3 | 4 | 5 | 6 | 7 | 8 | 9 | 10 |

FINISH
| SHORT | SHORT TO MED. | MEDIUM | MED. TO LONG | LONG |

NOTES

PRICE TO VALUE
| 1 | 2 | 3 | 4 | 5 | 6 | 7 | 8 | 9 | 10 |

OVERALL RATING
| 1 | 2 | 3 | 4 | 5 | 6 | 7 | 8 | 9 | 10 |

WINE _____ **DATE** _____

GRAPE _____ **VINTAGE** _____
PRODUCER _____ **REGION** _____
PRICE _____ **ALCHOOL %** _____

COLOR
| RED | WHITE | ROSE' | SPARKLING | EFFERVESCENT | FORTIFIED |

APPEARANCE
| THIN | TRANSLUCENT | SATURATED | OPAQUE |

BODY
| LIGHT | LIGHT TO MED. | MEDIUM | MED. TO FULL | FULL |

SMELL
- ☐ TOAST
- ☐ TOBACCO
- ☐ LEATHER
- ☐ MUSHROOM
- ☐ JAM
- ☐ CHOCOLATE
- ☐ COFFEE
- ☐ SMOKE
- ☐ PEPPER
- ☐ MINT
- ☐ SPICE
- ☐ ALMOND
- ☐ CITRUS
- ☐ MELON
- ☐ OAK
- ☐ BERRIES
- ☐ NUTMEG
- ☐ VEGETAL
- ☐ HONEY
- ☐ APPLE
- ☐ TROPICAL
- ☐ GRASS
- ☐ FLORAL
- ☐ BUTTER
- ☐ ....
- ☐ ....
- ☐ ....
- ☐ ....
- ☐ ....
- ☐ ....

TASTE
- ☐ DARK FRUIT
- ☐ BERRIES
- ☐ PLUMS
- ☐ MUSHROOM
- ☐ TOBACCO
- ☐ CHOCOLATE
- ☐ EARTH
- ☐ PEPPER
- ☐ VANILLA
- ☐ COFFEE
- ☐ LICORICE
- ☐ LEATHER
- ☐ TOAST
- ☐ GRASS
- ☐ CITRUS
- ☐ MELON
- ☐ LYCHEE
- ☐ ALMOND
- ☐ NUTMEG
- ☐ VEGETAL
- ☐ FLORAL
- ☐ HONEY
- ☐ PEARS
- ☐ PEACHES
- ☐ ....
- ☐ ....
- ☐ ....
- ☐ ....
- ☐ ....
- ☐ ....

DRY / SWEETNESS
| 1 | 2 | 3 | 4 | 5 | 6 | 7 | 8 | 9 | 10 |

BALANCE
| 1 | 2 | 3 | 4 | 5 | 6 | 7 | 8 | 9 | 10 |

TANNINS
| 1 | 2 | 3 | 4 | 5 | 6 | 7 | 8 | 9 | 10 |

FLOVOUR INTENSITY
| 1 | 2 | 3 | 4 | 5 | 6 | 7 | 8 | 9 | 10 |

FINISH
| SHORT | SHORT TO MED. | MEDIUM | MED. TO LONG | LONG |

NOTES

PRICE TO VALUE
| 1 | 2 | 3 | 4 | 5 | 6 | 7 | 8 | 9 | 10 |

OVERALL RATING
| 1 | 2 | 3 | 4 | 5 | 6 | 7 | 8 | 9 | 10 |

WINE _____ **DATE** _____

GRAPE _____ **VINTAGE** _____
PRODUCER _____ **REGION** _____
PRICE _____ **ALCHOOL %** _____

COLOR

RED	WHITE	ROSE'	SPARKLING	EFFERVESCENT	FORTIFIED

APPEARANCE

THIN	TRANSLUCENT	SATURATED	OPAQUE

BODY

LIGHT	LIGHT TO MED.	MEDIUM	MED. TO FULL	FULL

SMELL

- ☐ TOAST
- ☐ TOBACCO
- ☐ LEATHER
- ☐ MUSHROOM
- ☐ JAM
- ☐ CHOCOLATE
- ☐ COFFEE
- ☐ SMOKE
- ☐ PEPPER
- ☐ MINT
- ☐ SPICE
- ☐ ALMOND
- ☐ CITRUS
- ☐ MELON
- ☐ OAK
- ☐ BERRIES
- ☐ NUTMEG
- ☐ VEGETAL
- ☐ HONEY
- ☐ APPLE
- ☐ TROPICAL
- ☐ GRASS
- ☐ FLORAL
- ☐ BUTTER
- ☐ ....
- ☐ ....
- ☐ ....
- ☐ ....
- ☐ ....
- ☐ ....

TASTE

- ☐ DARK FRUIT
- ☐ BERRIES
- ☐ PLUMS
- ☐ MUSHROOM
- ☐ TOBACCO
- ☐ CHOCOLATE
- ☐ EARTH
- ☐ PEPPER
- ☐ VANILLA
- ☐ COFFEE
- ☐ LICORICE
- ☐ LEATHER
- ☐ TOAST
- ☐ GRASS
- ☐ CITRUS
- ☐ MELON
- ☐ LYCHEE
- ☐ ALMOND
- ☐ NUTMEG
- ☐ VEGETAL
- ☐ FLORAL
- ☐ HONEY
- ☐ PEARS
- ☐ PEACHES
- ☐ ....
- ☐ ....
- ☐ ....
- ☐ ....
- ☐ ....
- ☐ ....

DRY / SWEETNESS

1	2	3	4	5	6	7	8	9	10

BALANCE

1	2	3	4	5	6	7	8	9	10

TANNINS

1	2	3	4	5	6	7	8	9	10

FLOVOUR INTENSITY

1	2	3	4	5	6	7	8	9	10

FINISH

SHORT	SHORT TO MED.	MEDIUM	MED. TO LONG	LONG

NOTES

PRICE TO VALUE

1	2	3	4	5	6	7	8	9	10

OVERALL RATING

1	2	3	4	5	6	7	8	9	10

WINE _____   **DATE** _____

GRAPE _____   **VINTAGE** _____
PRODUCER _____   **REGION** _____
PRICE _____   **ALCHOOL %** _____

COLOR

| RED | WHITE | ROSE' | SPARKLING | EFFERVESCENT | FORTIFIED |

APPEARANCE

| THIN | TRANSLUCENT | SATURATED | OPAQUE |

BODY

| LIGHT | LIGHT TO MED. | MEDIUM | MED. TO FULL | FULL |

SMELL

- ☐ TOAST
- ☐ TOBACCO
- ☐ LEATHER
- ☐ MUSHROOM
- ☐ JAM
- ☐ CHOCOLATE
- ☐ COFFEE
- ☐ SMOKE
- ☐ PEPPER
- ☐ MINT
- ☐ SPICE
- ☐ ALMOND
- ☐ CITRUS
- ☐ MELON
- ☐ OAK
- ☐ BERRIES
- ☐ NUTMEG
- ☐ VEGETAL
- ☐ HONEY
- ☐ APPLE
- ☐ TROPICAL
- ☐ GRASS
- ☐ FLORAL
- ☐ BUTTER
- ☐ ....
- ☐ ....
- ☐ ....
- ☐ ....
- ☐ ....
- ☐ ....

TASTE

- ☐ DARK FRUIT
- ☐ BERRIES
- ☐ PLUMS
- ☐ MUSHROOM
- ☐ TOBACCO
- ☐ CHOCOLATE
- ☐ EARTH
- ☐ PEPPER
- ☐ VANILLA
- ☐ COFFEE
- ☐ LICORICE
- ☐ LEATHER
- ☐ TOAST
- ☐ GRASS
- ☐ CITRUS
- ☐ MELON
- ☐ LYCHEE
- ☐ ALMOND
- ☐ NUTMEG
- ☐ VEGETAL
- ☐ FLORAL
- ☐ HONEY
- ☐ PEARS
- ☐ PEACHES
- ☐ ....
- ☐ ....
- ☐ ....
- ☐ ....
- ☐ ....
- ☐ ....

DRY / SWEETNESS
| 1 | 2 | 3 | 4 | 5 | 6 | 7 | 8 | 9 | 10 |

BALANCE
| 1 | 2 | 3 | 4 | 5 | 6 | 7 | 8 | 9 | 10 |

TANNINS
| 1 | 2 | 3 | 4 | 5 | 6 | 7 | 8 | 9 | 10 |

FLOVOUR INTENSITY
| 1 | 2 | 3 | 4 | 5 | 6 | 7 | 8 | 9 | 10 |

FINISH

| SHORT | SHORT TO MED. | MEDIUM | MED. TO LONG | LONG |

NOTES

PRICE TO VALUE
| 1 | 2 | 3 | 4 | 5 | 6 | 7 | 8 | 9 | 10 |

OVERALL RATING
| 1 | 2 | 3 | 4 | 5 | 6 | 7 | 8 | 9 | 10 |

WINE		DATE	
GRAPE		VINTAGE	
PRODUCER		REGION	
PRICE		ALCHOOL %	

COLOR

RED	WHITE	ROSE	SPARKLING	EFFERVESCENT	FORTIFIED

APPEARANCE

THIN	TRANSLUCENT	SATURATED	OPAQUE

BODY

LIGHT	LIGHT TO MED.	MEDIUM	MED. TO FULL	FULL

SMELL

- ☐ TOAST
- ☐ TOBACCO
- ☐ LEATHER
- ☐ MUSHROOM
- ☐ JAM
- ☐ CHOCOLATE
- ☐ COFFEE
- ☐ SMOKE
- ☐ PEPPER
- ☐ MINT
- ☐ SPICE
- ☐ ALMOND
- ☐ CITRUS
- ☐ MELON
- ☐ OAK
- ☐ BERRIES
- ☐ NUTMEG
- ☐ VEGETAL
- ☐ HONEY
- ☐ APPLE
- ☐ TROPICAL
- ☐ GRASS
- ☐ FLORAL
- ☐ BUTTER
- ☐ ....
- ☐ ....
- ☐ ....
- ☐ ....
- ☐ ....
- ☐ ....

TASTE

- ☐ DARK FRUIT
- ☐ BERRIES
- ☐ PLUMS
- ☐ MUSHROOM
- ☐ TOBACCO
- ☐ CHOCOLATE
- ☐ EARTH
- ☐ PEPPER
- ☐ VANILLA
- ☐ COFFEE
- ☐ LICORICE
- ☐ LEATHER
- ☐ TOAST
- ☐ GRASS
- ☐ CITRUS
- ☐ MELON
- ☐ LYCHEE
- ☐ ALMOND
- ☐ NUTMEG
- ☐ VEGETAL
- ☐ FLORAL
- ☐ HONEY
- ☐ PEARS
- ☐ PEACHES
- ☐ ....
- ☐ ....
- ☐ ....
- ☐ ....
- ☐ ....
- ☐ ....

DRY / SWEETNESS

1	2	3	4	5	6	7	8	9	10

BALANCE

1	2	3	4	5	6	7	8	9	10

TANNINS

1	2	3	4	5	6	7	8	9	10

FLOVOUR INTENSITY

1	2	3	4	5	6	7	8	9	10

FINISH

SHORT	SHORT TO MED.	MEDIUM	MED. TO LONG	LONG

NOTES

PRICE TO VALUE

1	2	3	4	5	6	7	8	9	10

OVERALL RATING

1	2	3	4	5	6	7	8	9	10

WINE	DATE
GRAPE	VINTAGE
PRODUCER	REGION
PRICE	ALCHOOL %

COLOR

RED	WHITE	ROSE	SPARKLING	EFFERVESCENT	FORTIFIED

APPEARANCE

THIN	TRANSLUCENT	SATURATED	OPAQUE

BODY

LIGHT	LIGHT TO MED.	MEDIUM	MED. TO FULL	FULL

SMELL

- ☐ TOAST
- ☐ TOBACCO
- ☐ LEATHER
- ☐ MUSHROOM
- ☐ JAM
- ☐ CHOCOLATE
- ☐ COFFEE
- ☐ SMOKE
- ☐ PEPPER
- ☐ MINT
- ☐ SPICE
- ☐ ALMOND
- ☐ CITRUS
- ☐ MELON
- ☐ OAK
- ☐ BERRIES
- ☐ NUTMEG
- ☐ VEGETAL
- ☐ HONEY
- ☐ APPLE
- ☐ TROPICAL
- ☐ GRASS
- ☐ FLORAL
- ☐ BUTTER
- ☐ ....
- ☐ ....
- ☐ ....
- ☐ ....
- ☐ ....
- ☐ ....

TASTE

- ☐ DARK FRUIT
- ☐ BERRIES
- ☐ PLUMS
- ☐ MUSHROOM
- ☐ TOBACCO
- ☐ CHOCOLATE
- ☐ EARTH
- ☐ PEPPER
- ☐ VANILLA
- ☐ COFFEE
- ☐ LICORICE
- ☐ LEATHER
- ☐ TOAST
- ☐ GRASS
- ☐ CITRUS
- ☐ MELON
- ☐ LYCHEE
- ☐ ALMOND
- ☐ NUTMEG
- ☐ VEGETAL
- ☐ FLORAL
- ☐ HONEY
- ☐ PEARS
- ☐ PEACHES
- ☐ ....
- ☐ ....
- ☐ ....
- ☐ ....
- ☐ ....
- ☐ ....

DRY / SWEETNESS
1	2	3	4	5	6	7	8	9	10

BALANCE
1	2	3	4	5	6	7	8	9	10

TANNINS
1	2	3	4	5	6	7	8	9	10

FLOVOUR INTENSITY
1	2	3	4	5	6	7	8	9	10

FINISH

SHORT	SHORT TO MED.	MEDIUM	MED. TO LONG	LONG

NOTES

PRICE TO VALUE
1	2	3	4	5	6	7	8	9	10

OVERALL RATING
1	2	3	4	5	6	7	8	9	10

WINE		DATE	
GRAPE		**VINTAGE**	
PRODUCER		**REGION**	
PRICE		**ALCHOOL %**	

COLOR

RED	WHITE	ROSE'	SPARKLING	EFFERVESCENT	FORTIFIED

APPEARANCE

THIN	TRANSLUCENT	SATURATED	OPAQUE

BODY

LIGHT	LIGHT TO MED.	MEDIUM	MED. TO FULL	FULL

SMELL

- ☐ TOAST
- ☐ TOBACCO
- ☐ LEATHER
- ☐ MUSHROOM
- ☐ JAM
- ☐ CHOCOLATE
- ☐ COFFEE
- ☐ SMOKE
- ☐ PEPPER
- ☐ MINT
- ☐ SPICE
- ☐ ALMOND
- ☐ CITRUS
- ☐ MELON
- ☐ OAK
- ☐ BERRIES
- ☐ NUTMEG
- ☐ VEGETAL
- ☐ HONEY
- ☐ APPLE
- ☐ TROPICAL
- ☐ GRASS
- ☐ FLORAL
- ☐ BUTTER
- ☐ ....
- ☐ ....
- ☐ ....
- ☐ ....
- ☐ ....
- ☐ ....

TASTE

- ☐ DARK FRUIT
- ☐ BERRIES
- ☐ PLUMS
- ☐ MUSHROOM
- ☐ TOBACCO
- ☐ CHOCOLATE
- ☐ EARTH
- ☐ PEPPER
- ☐ VANILLA
- ☐ COFFEE
- ☐ LICORICE
- ☐ LEATHER
- ☐ TOAST
- ☐ GRASS
- ☐ CITRUS
- ☐ MELON
- ☐ LYCHEE
- ☐ ALMOND
- ☐ NUTMEG
- ☐ VEGETAL
- ☐ FLORAL
- ☐ HONEY
- ☐ PEARS
- ☐ PEACHES
- ☐ ....
- ☐ ....
- ☐ ....
- ☐ ....
- ☐ ....
- ☐ ....

DRY / SWEETNESS
1	2	3	4	5	6	7	8	9	10

BALANCE
1	2	3	4	5	6	7	8	9	10

TANNINS
1	2	3	4	5	6	7	8	9	10

FLOVOUR INTENSITY
1	2	3	4	5	6	7	8	9	10

FINISH

SHORT	SHORT TO MED.	MEDIUM	MED. TO LONG	LONG

NOTES

PRICE TO VALUE
1	2	3	4	5	6	7	8	9	10

OVERALL RATING
1	2	3	4	5	6	7	8	9	10

WINE   **DATE**

GRAPE   **VINTAGE**
PRODUCER   **REGION**
PRICE   **ALCHOOL %**

COLOR

RED	WHITE	ROSE'	SPARKLING	EFFERVESCENT	FORTIFIED

APPEARANCE

THIN	TRANSLUCENT	SATURATED	OPAQUE

BODY

LIGHT	LIGHT TO MED.	MEDIUM	MED. TO FULL	FULL

SMELL

- ☐ TOAST
- ☐ TOBACCO
- ☐ LEATHER
- ☐ MUSHROOM
- ☐ JAM
- ☐ CHOCOLATE
- ☐ COFFEE
- ☐ SMOKE
- ☐ PEPPER
- ☐ MINT
- ☐ SPICE
- ☐ ALMOND
- ☐ CITRUS
- ☐ MELON
- ☐ OAK
- ☐ BERRIES
- ☐ NUTMEG
- ☐ VEGETAL
- ☐ HONEY
- ☐ APPLE
- ☐ TROPICAL
- ☐ GRASS
- ☐ FLORAL
- ☐ BUTTER
- ☐ ....
- ☐ ....
- ☐ ....
- ☐ ....
- ☐ ....
- ☐ ....

TASTE

- ☐ DARK FRUIT
- ☐ BERRIES
- ☐ PLUMS
- ☐ MUSHROOM
- ☐ TOBACCO
- ☐ CHOCOLATE
- ☐ EARTH
- ☐ PEPPER
- ☐ VANILLA
- ☐ COFFEE
- ☐ LICORICE
- ☐ LEATHER
- ☐ TOAST
- ☐ GRASS
- ☐ CITRUS
- ☐ MELON
- ☐ LYCHEE
- ☐ ALMOND
- ☐ NUTMEG
- ☐ VEGETAL
- ☐ FLORAL
- ☐ HONEY
- ☐ PEARS
- ☐ PEACHES
- ☐ ....
- ☐ ....
- ☐ ....
- ☐ ....
- ☐ ....
- ☐ ....

DRY / SWEETNESS

1	2	3	4	5	6	7	8	9	10

BALANCE

1	2	3	4	5	6	7	8	9	10

TANNINS

1	2	3	4	5	6	7	8	9	10

FLOVOUR INTENSITY

1	2	3	4	5	6	7	8	9	10

FINISH

SHORT	SHORT TO MED.	MEDIUM	MED. TO LONG	LONG

NOTES

PRICE TO VALUE

1	2	3	4	5	6	7	8	9	10

OVERALL RATING

1	2	3	4	5	6	7	8	9	10

WINE		DATE	
GRAPE		VINTAGE	
PRODUCER		REGION	
PRICE		ALCHOOL %	

COLOR

RED	WHITE	ROSE'	SPARKLING	EFFERVESCENT	FORTIFIED

APPEARANCE

THIN	TRANSLUCENT	SATURATED	OPAQUE

BODY

LIGHT	LIGHT TO MED.	MEDIUM	MED. TO FULL	FULL

SMELL

- ☐ TOAST
- ☐ TOBACCO
- ☐ LEATHER
- ☐ MUSHROOM
- ☐ JAM
- ☐ CHOCOLATE
- ☐ COFFEE
- ☐ SMOKE
- ☐ PEPPER
- ☐ MINT
- ☐ SPICE
- ☐ ALMOND
- ☐ CITRUS
- ☐ MELON
- ☐ OAK
- ☐ BERRIES
- ☐ NUTMEG
- ☐ VEGETAL
- ☐ HONEY
- ☐ APPLE
- ☐ TROPICAL
- ☐ GRASS
- ☐ FLORAL
- ☐ BUTTER
- ☐ ....
- ☐ ....
- ☐ ....
- ☐ ....
- ☐ ....
- ☐ ....

TASTE

- ☐ DARK FRUIT
- ☐ BERRIES
- ☐ PLUMS
- ☐ MUSHROOM
- ☐ TOBACCO
- ☐ CHOCOLATE
- ☐ EARTH
- ☐ PEPPER
- ☐ VANILLA
- ☐ COFFEE
- ☐ LICORICE
- ☐ LEATHER
- ☐ TOAST
- ☐ GRASS
- ☐ CITRUS
- ☐ MELON
- ☐ LYCHEE
- ☐ ALMOND
- ☐ NUTMEG
- ☐ VEGETAL
- ☐ FLORAL
- ☐ HONEY
- ☐ PEARS
- ☐ PEACHES
- ☐ ....
- ☐ ....
- ☐ ....
- ☐ ....
- ☐ ....
- ☐ ....

DRY / SWEETNESS

1	2	3	4	5	6	7	8	9	10

BALANCE

1	2	3	4	5	6	7	8	9	10

TANNINS

1	2	3	4	5	6	7	8	9	10

FLOVOUR INTENSITY

1	2	3	4	5	6	7	8	9	10

FINISH

SHORT	SHORT TO MED.	MEDIUM	MED. TO LONG	LONG

NOTES

PRICE TO VALUE

1	2	3	4	5	6	7	8	9	10

OVERALL RATING

1	2	3	4	5	6	7	8	9	10

WINE   **DATE**

GRAPE   **VINTAGE**
PRODUCER   **REGION**
PRICE   **ALCHOOL %**

COLOR

| RED | WHITE | ROSE | SPARKLING | EFFERVESCENT | FORTIFIED |

APPEARANCE

| THIN | TRANSLUCENT | SATURATED | OPAQUE |

BODY

| LIGHT | LIGHT TO MED. | MEDIUM | MED. TO FULL | FULL |

SMELL

- ☐ TOAST
- ☐ TOBACCO
- ☐ LEATHER
- ☐ MUSHROOM
- ☐ JAM
- ☐ CHOCOLATE
- ☐ COFFEE
- ☐ SMOKE
- ☐ PEPPER
- ☐ MINT
- ☐ SPICE
- ☐ ALMOND
- ☐ CITRUS
- ☐ MELON
- ☐ OAK
- ☐ BERRIES
- ☐ NUTMEG
- ☐ VEGETAL
- ☐ HONEY
- ☐ APPLE
- ☐ TROPICAL
- ☐ GRASS
- ☐ FLORAL
- ☐ BUTTER
- ☐ ....
- ☐ ....
- ☐ ....
- ☐ ....
- ☐ ....
- ☐ ....

TASTE

- ☐ DARK FRUIT
- ☐ BERRIES
- ☐ PLUMS
- ☐ MUSHROOM
- ☐ TOBACCO
- ☐ CHOCOLATE
- ☐ EARTH
- ☐ PEPPER
- ☐ VANILLA
- ☐ COFFEE
- ☐ LICORICE
- ☐ LEATHER
- ☐ TOAST
- ☐ GRASS
- ☐ CITRUS
- ☐ MELON
- ☐ LYCHEE
- ☐ ALMOND
- ☐ NUTMEG
- ☐ VEGETAL
- ☐ FLORAL
- ☐ HONEY
- ☐ PEARS
- ☐ PEACHES
- ☐ ....
- ☐ ....
- ☐ ....
- ☐ ....
- ☐ ....
- ☐ ....

DRY / SWEETNESS

| 1 | 2 | 3 | 4 | 5 | 6 | 7 | 8 | 9 | 10 |

BALANCE

| 1 | 2 | 3 | 4 | 5 | 6 | 7 | 8 | 9 | 10 |

TANNINS

| 1 | 2 | 3 | 4 | 5 | 6 | 7 | 8 | 9 | 10 |

FLOVOUR INTENSITY

| 1 | 2 | 3 | 4 | 5 | 6 | 7 | 8 | 9 | 10 |

FINISH

| SHORT | SHORT TO MED. | MEDIUM | MED. TO LONG | LONG |

NOTES

PRICE TO VALUE

| 1 | 2 | 3 | 4 | 5 | 6 | 7 | 8 | 9 | 10 |

OVERALL RATING

| 1 | 2 | 3 | 4 | 5 | 6 | 7 | 8 | 9 | 10 |

WINE _____ **DATE** _____

GRAPE _____ **VINTAGE** _____
PRODUCER _____ **REGION** _____
PRICE _____ **ALCHOOL %** _____

COLOR

| RED | WHITE | ROSE | SPARKLING | EFFERVESCENT | FORTIFIED |

APPEARANCE

| THIN | TRANSLUCENT | SATURATED | OPAQUE |

BODY

| LIGHT | LIGHT TO MED. | MEDIUM | MED. TO FULL | FULL |

SMELL

- ☐ TOAST
- ☐ TOBACCO
- ☐ LEATHER
- ☐ MUSHROOM
- ☐ JAM
- ☐ CHOCOLATE
- ☐ COFFEE
- ☐ SMOKE
- ☐ PEPPER
- ☐ MINT
- ☐ SPICE
- ☐ ALMOND
- ☐ CITRUS
- ☐ MELON
- ☐ OAK
- ☐ BERRIES
- ☐ NUTMEG
- ☐ VEGETAL
- ☐ HONEY
- ☐ APPLE
- ☐ TROPICAL
- ☐ GRASS
- ☐ FLORAL
- ☐ BUTTER
- ☐ ....
- ☐ ....
- ☐ ....
- ☐ ....
- ☐ ....
- ☐ ....

TASTE

- ☐ DARK FRUIT
- ☐ BERRIES
- ☐ PLUMS
- ☐ MUSHROOM
- ☐ TOBACCO
- ☐ CHOCOLATE
- ☐ EARTH
- ☐ PEPPER
- ☐ VANILLA
- ☐ COFFEE
- ☐ LICORICE
- ☐ LEATHER
- ☐ TOAST
- ☐ GRASS
- ☐ CITRUS
- ☐ MELON
- ☐ LYCHEE
- ☐ ALMOND
- ☐ NUTMEG
- ☐ VEGETAL
- ☐ FLORAL
- ☐ HONEY
- ☐ PEARS
- ☐ PEACHES
- ☐ ....
- ☐ ....
- ☐ ....
- ☐ ....
- ☐ ....
- ☐ ....

DRY / SWEETNESS
| 1 | 2 | 3 | 4 | 5 | 6 | 7 | 8 | 9 | 10 |

BALANCE
| 1 | 2 | 3 | 4 | 5 | 6 | 7 | 8 | 9 | 10 |

TANNINS
| 1 | 2 | 3 | 4 | 5 | 6 | 7 | 8 | 9 | 10 |

FLOVOUR INTENSITY
| 1 | 2 | 3 | 4 | 5 | 6 | 7 | 8 | 9 | 10 |

FINISH

| SHORT | SHORT TO MED. | MEDIUM | MED. TO LONG | LONG |

NOTES
_____
_____
_____
_____
_____
_____

PRICE TO VALUE
| 1 | 2 | 3 | 4 | 5 | 6 | 7 | 8 | 9 | 10 |

OVERALL RATING
| 1 | 2 | 3 | 4 | 5 | 6 | 7 | 8 | 9 | 10 |

WINE		DATE	
GRAPE		**VINTAGE**	
PRODUCER		**REGION**	
PRICE		**ALCHOOL %**	

COLOR

RED	WHITE	ROSE'	SPARKLING	EFFERVESCENT	FORTIFIED

APPEARANCE

THIN	TRANSLUCENT	SATURATED	OPAQUE

BODY

LIGHT	LIGHT TO MED.	MEDIUM	MED. TO FULL	FULL

SMELL

- ☐ TOAST
- ☐ TOBACCO
- ☐ LEATHER
- ☐ MUSHROOM
- ☐ JAM
- ☐ CHOCOLATE
- ☐ COFFEE
- ☐ SMOKE
- ☐ PEPPER
- ☐ MINT
- ☐ SPICE
- ☐ ALMOND
- ☐ CITRUS
- ☐ MELON
- ☐ OAK
- ☐ BERRIES
- ☐ NUTMEG
- ☐ VEGETAL
- ☐ HONEY
- ☐ APPLE
- ☐ TROPICAL
- ☐ GRASS
- ☐ FLORAL
- ☐ BUTTER
- ☐ ....
- ☐ ....
- ☐ ....
- ☐ ....
- ☐ ....
- ☐ ....

TASTE

- ☐ DARK FRUIT
- ☐ BERRIES
- ☐ PLUMS
- ☐ MUSHROOM
- ☐ TOBACCO
- ☐ CHOCOLATE
- ☐ EARTH
- ☐ PEPPER
- ☐ VANILLA
- ☐ COFFEE
- ☐ LICORICE
- ☐ LEATHER
- ☐ TOAST
- ☐ GRASS
- ☐ CITRUS
- ☐ MELON
- ☐ LYCHEE
- ☐ ALMOND
- ☐ NUTMEG
- ☐ VEGETAL
- ☐ FLORAL
- ☐ HONEY
- ☐ PEARS
- ☐ PEACHES
- ☐ ....
- ☐ ....
- ☐ ....
- ☐ ....
- ☐ ....
- ☐ ....

DRY / SWEETNESS
1	2	3	4	5	6	7	8	9	10

BALANCE
1	2	3	4	5	6	7	8	9	10

TANNINS
1	2	3	4	5	6	7	8	9	10

FLOVOUR INTENSITY
1	2	3	4	5	6	7	8	9	10

FINISH

SHORT	SHORT TO MED.	MEDIUM	MED. TO LONG	LONG

NOTES

PRICE TO VALUE
1	2	3	4	5	6	7	8	9	10

OVERALL RATING
1	2	3	4	5	6	7	8	9	10

WINE _____ **DATE** _____

GRAPE _____ **VINTAGE** _____
PRODUCER _____ **REGION** _____
PRICE _____ **ALCHOOL %** _____

COLOR

| RED | WHITE | ROSE' | SPARKLING | EFFERVESCENT | FORTIFIED |

APPEARANCE

| THIN | TRANSLUCENT | SATURATED | OPAQUE |

BODY

| LIGHT | LIGHT TO MED. | MEDIUM | MED. TO FULL | FULL |

SMELL

- ☐ TOAST
- ☐ TOBACCO
- ☐ LEATHER
- ☐ MUSHROOM
- ☐ JAM
- ☐ CHOCOLATE
- ☐ COFFEE
- ☐ SMOKE
- ☐ PEPPER
- ☐ MINT
- ☐ SPICE
- ☐ ALMOND
- ☐ CITRUS
- ☐ MELON
- ☐ OAK
- ☐ BERRIES
- ☐ NUTMEG
- ☐ VEGETAL
- ☐ HONEY
- ☐ APPLE
- ☐ TROPICAL
- ☐ GRASS
- ☐ FLORAL
- ☐ BUTTER
- ☐ _____
- ☐ _____
- ☐ _____
- ☐ _____
- ☐ _____
- ☐ _____

TASTE

- ☐ DARK FRUIT
- ☐ BERRIES
- ☐ PLUMS
- ☐ MUSHROOM
- ☐ TOBACCO
- ☐ CHOCOLATE
- ☐ EARTH
- ☐ PEPPER
- ☐ VANILLA
- ☐ COFFEE
- ☐ LICORICE
- ☐ LEATHER
- ☐ TOAST
- ☐ GRASS
- ☐ CITRUS
- ☐ MELON
- ☐ LYCHEE
- ☐ ALMOND
- ☐ NUTMEG
- ☐ VEGETAL
- ☐ FLORAL
- ☐ HONEY
- ☐ PEARS
- ☐ PEACHES
- ☐ _____
- ☐ _____
- ☐ _____
- ☐ _____
- ☐ _____
- ☐ _____

DRY / SWEETNESS
| 1 | 2 | 3 | 4 | 5 | 6 | 7 | 8 | 9 | 10 |

BALANCE
| 1 | 2 | 3 | 4 | 5 | 6 | 7 | 8 | 9 | 10 |

TANNINS
| 1 | 2 | 3 | 4 | 5 | 6 | 7 | 8 | 9 | 10 |

FLOVOUR INTENSITY
| 1 | 2 | 3 | 4 | 5 | 6 | 7 | 8 | 9 | 10 |

FINISH

| SHORT | SHORT TO MED. | MEDIUM | MED. TO LONG | LONG |

NOTES

PRICE TO VALUE
| 1 | 2 | 3 | 4 | 5 | 6 | 7 | 8 | 9 | 10 |

OVERALL RATING
| 1 | 2 | 3 | 4 | 5 | 6 | 7 | 8 | 9 | 10 |

WINE _____ **DATE** _____

GRAPE _____ **VINTAGE** _____
PRODUCER _____ **REGION** _____
PRICE _____ **ALCHOOL %** _____

COLOR

| RED | WHITE | ROSE' | SPARKLING | EFFERVESCENT | FORTIFIED |

APPEARANCE

| THIN | TRANSLUCENT | SATURATED | OPAQUE |

BODY

| LIGHT | LIGHT TO MED. | MEDIUM | MED. TO FULL | FULL |

SMELL

- ☐ TOAST
- ☐ TOBACCO
- ☐ LEATHER
- ☐ MUSHROOM
- ☐ JAM
- ☐ CHOCOLATE
- ☐ COFFEE
- ☐ SMOKE
- ☐ PEPPER
- ☐ MINT
- ☐ SPICE
- ☐ ALMOND
- ☐ CITRUS
- ☐ MELON
- ☐ OAK
- ☐ BERRIES
- ☐ NUTMEG
- ☐ VEGETAL
- ☐ HONEY
- ☐ APPLE
- ☐ TROPICAL
- ☐ GRASS
- ☐ FLORAL
- ☐ BUTTER
- ☐ ....
- ☐ ....
- ☐ ....
- ☐ ....
- ☐ ....
- ☐ ....

TASTE

- ☐ DARK FRUIT
- ☐ BERRIES
- ☐ PLUMS
- ☐ MUSHROOM
- ☐ TOBACCO
- ☐ CHOCOLATE
- ☐ EARTH
- ☐ PEPPER
- ☐ VANILLA
- ☐ COFFEE
- ☐ LICORICE
- ☐ LEATHER
- ☐ TOAST
- ☐ GRASS
- ☐ CITRUS
- ☐ MELON
- ☐ LYCHEE
- ☐ ALMOND
- ☐ NUTMEG
- ☐ VEGETAL
- ☐ FLORAL
- ☐ HONEY
- ☐ PEARS
- ☐ PEACHES
- ☐ ....
- ☐ ....
- ☐ ....
- ☐ ....
- ☐ ....
- ☐ ....

DRY / SWEETNESS
| 1 | 2 | 3 | 4 | 5 | 6 | 7 | 8 | 9 | 10 |

BALANCE
| 1 | 2 | 3 | 4 | 5 | 6 | 7 | 8 | 9 | 10 |

TANNINS
| 1 | 2 | 3 | 4 | 5 | 6 | 7 | 8 | 9 | 10 |

FLOVOUR INTENSITY
| 1 | 2 | 3 | 4 | 5 | 6 | 7 | 8 | 9 | 10 |

FINISH

| SHORT | SHORT TO MED. | MEDIUM | MED. TO LONG | LONG |

NOTES _____
_____
_____
_____
_____

PRICE TO VALUE
| 1 | 2 | 3 | 4 | 5 | 6 | 7 | 8 | 9 | 10 |

OVERALL RATING
| 1 | 2 | 3 | 4 | 5 | 6 | 7 | 8 | 9 | 10 |

WINE _____   **DATE** _____

GRAPE _____   **VINTAGE** _____
PRODUCER _____   **REGION** _____
PRICE _____   **ALCHOOL %** _____

COLOR

| RED | WHITE | ROSE' | SPARKLING | EFFERVESCENT | FORTIFIED |

APPEARANCE

| THIN | TRANSLUCENT | SATURATED | OPAQUE |

BODY

| LIGHT | LIGHT TO MED. | MEDIUM | MED. TO FULL | FULL |

SMELL

- ☐ TOAST
- ☐ TOBACCO
- ☐ LEATHER
- ☐ MUSHROOM
- ☐ JAM
- ☐ CHOCOLATE
- ☐ COFFEE
- ☐ SMOKE
- ☐ PEPPER
- ☐ MINT
- ☐ SPICE
- ☐ ALMOND
- ☐ CITRUS
- ☐ MELON
- ☐ OAK
- ☐ BERRIES
- ☐ NUTMEG
- ☐ VEGETAL
- ☐ HONEY
- ☐ APPLE
- ☐ TROPICAL
- ☐ GRASS
- ☐ FLORAL
- ☐ BUTTER
- ☐ ....
- ☐ ....
- ☐ ....
- ☐ ....
- ☐ ....
- ☐ ....

TASTE

- ☐ DARK FRUIT
- ☐ BERRIES
- ☐ PLUMS
- ☐ MUSHROOM
- ☐ TOBACCO
- ☐ CHOCOLATE
- ☐ EARTH
- ☐ PEPPER
- ☐ VANILLA
- ☐ COFFEE
- ☐ LICORICE
- ☐ LEATHER
- ☐ TOAST
- ☐ GRASS
- ☐ CITRUS
- ☐ MELON
- ☐ LYCHEE
- ☐ ALMOND
- ☐ NUTMEG
- ☐ VEGETAL
- ☐ FLORAL
- ☐ HONEY
- ☐ PEARS
- ☐ PEACHES
- ☐ ....
- ☐ ....
- ☐ ....
- ☐ ....
- ☐ ....
- ☐ ....

DRY / SWEETNESS
| 1 | 2 | 3 | 4 | 5 | 6 | 7 | 8 | 9 | 10 |

BALANCE
| 1 | 2 | 3 | 4 | 5 | 6 | 7 | 8 | 9 | 10 |

TANNINS
| 1 | 2 | 3 | 4 | 5 | 6 | 7 | 8 | 9 | 10 |

FLOVOUR INTENSITY
| 1 | 2 | 3 | 4 | 5 | 6 | 7 | 8 | 9 | 10 |

FINISH

| SHORT | SHORT TO MED. | MEDIUM | MED. TO LONG | LONG |

NOTES
_____
_____
_____
_____

PRICE TO VALUE
| 1 | 2 | 3 | 4 | 5 | 6 | 7 | 8 | 9 | 10 |

OVERALL RATING
| 1 | 2 | 3 | 4 | 5 | 6 | 7 | 8 | 9 | 10 |

WINE _____ **DATE** _____

GRAPE _____ **VINTAGE** _____
PRODUCER _____ **REGION** _____
PRICE _____ **ALCHOOL %** _____

COLOR

| RED | WHITE | ROSE | SPARKLING | EFFERVESCENT | FORTIFIED |

APPEARANCE

| THIN | TRANSLUCENT | SATURATED | OPAQUE |

BODY

| LIGHT | LIGHT TO MED. | MEDIUM | MED. TO FULL | FULL |

SMELL

- ☐ TOAST
- ☐ TOBACCO
- ☐ LEATHER
- ☐ MUSHROOM
- ☐ JAM
- ☐ CHOCOLATE
- ☐ COFFEE
- ☐ SMOKE
- ☐ PEPPER
- ☐ MINT
- ☐ SPICE
- ☐ ALMOND
- ☐ CITRUS
- ☐ MELON
- ☐ OAK
- ☐ BERRIES
- ☐ NUTMEG
- ☐ VEGETAL
- ☐ HONEY
- ☐ APPLE
- ☐ TROPICAL
- ☐ GRASS
- ☐ FLORAL
- ☐ BUTTER
- ☐ ....
- ☐ ....
- ☐ ....
- ☐ ....
- ☐ ....
- ☐ ....

TASTE

- ☐ DARK FRUIT
- ☐ BERRIES
- ☐ PLUMS
- ☐ MUSHROOM
- ☐ TOBACCO
- ☐ CHOCOLATE
- ☐ EARTH
- ☐ PEPPER
- ☐ VANILLA
- ☐ COFFEE
- ☐ LICORICE
- ☐ LEATHER
- ☐ TOAST
- ☐ GRASS
- ☐ CITRUS
- ☐ MELON
- ☐ LYCHEE
- ☐ ALMOND
- ☐ NUTMEG
- ☐ VEGETAL
- ☐ FLORAL
- ☐ HONEY
- ☐ PEARS
- ☐ PEACHES
- ☐ ....
- ☐ ....
- ☐ ....
- ☐ ....
- ☐ ....
- ☐ ....

DRY / SWEETNESS
| 1 | 2 | 3 | 4 | 5 | 6 | 7 | 8 | 9 | 10 |

BALANCE
| 1 | 2 | 3 | 4 | 5 | 6 | 7 | 8 | 9 | 10 |

TANNINS
| 1 | 2 | 3 | 4 | 5 | 6 | 7 | 8 | 9 | 10 |

FLOVOUR INTENSITY
| 1 | 2 | 3 | 4 | 5 | 6 | 7 | 8 | 9 | 10 |

FINISH

| SHORT | SHORT TO MED. | MEDIUM | MED. TO LONG | LONG |

NOTES

PRICE TO VALUE
| 1 | 2 | 3 | 4 | 5 | 6 | 7 | 8 | 9 | 10 |

OVERALL RATING
| 1 | 2 | 3 | 4 | 5 | 6 | 7 | 8 | 9 | 10 |

WINE _____ **DATE** _____

GRAPE _____ **VINTAGE** _____
PRODUCER _____ **REGION** _____
PRICE _____ **ALCHOOL %** _____

COLOR

RED	WHITE	ROSE	SPARKLING	EFFERVESCENT	FORTIFIED

APPEARANCE

THIN	TRANSLUCENT	SATURATED	OPAQUE

BODY

LIGHT	LIGHT TO MED.	MEDIUM	MED. TO FULL	FULL

SMELL

- ☐ TOAST
- ☐ TOBACCO
- ☐ LEATHER
- ☐ MUSHROOM
- ☐ JAM
- ☐ CHOCOLATE
- ☐ COFFEE
- ☐ SMOKE
- ☐ PEPPER
- ☐ MINT
- ☐ SPICE
- ☐ ALMOND
- ☐ CITRUS
- ☐ MELON
- ☐ OAK
- ☐ BERRIES
- ☐ NUTMEG
- ☐ VEGETAL
- ☐ HONEY
- ☐ APPLE
- ☐ TROPICAL
- ☐ GRASS
- ☐ FLORAL
- ☐ BUTTER
- ☐ ....
- ☐ ....
- ☐ ....
- ☐ ....
- ☐ ....
- ☐ ....

TASTE

- ☐ DARK FRUIT
- ☐ BERRIES
- ☐ PLUMS
- ☐ MUSHROOM
- ☐ TOBACCO
- ☐ CHOCOLATE
- ☐ EARTH
- ☐ PEPPER
- ☐ VANILLA
- ☐ COFFEE
- ☐ LICORICE
- ☐ LEATHER
- ☐ TOAST
- ☐ GRASS
- ☐ CITRUS
- ☐ MELON
- ☐ LYCHEE
- ☐ ALMOND
- ☐ NUTMEG
- ☐ VEGETAL
- ☐ FLORAL
- ☐ HONEY
- ☐ PEARS
- ☐ PEACHES
- ☐ ....
- ☐ ....
- ☐ ....
- ☐ ....
- ☐ ....
- ☐ ....

DRY / SWEETNESS

1	2	3	4	5	6	7	8	9	10

BALANCE

1	2	3	4	5	6	7	8	9	10

TANNINS

1	2	3	4	5	6	7	8	9	10

FLOVOUR INTENSITY

1	2	3	4	5	6	7	8	9	10

FINISH

SHORT	SHORT TO MED.	MEDIUM	MED. TO LONG	LONG

NOTES

_____
_____
_____
_____
_____

PRICE TO VALUE

1	2	3	4	5	6	7	8	9	10

OVERALL RATING

1	2	3	4	5	6	7	8	9	10

WINE		DATE	
GRAPE		**VINTAGE**	
PRODUCER		**REGION**	
PRICE		**ALCHOOL %**	

COLOR

RED	WHITE	ROSE	SPARKLING	EFFERVESCENT	FORTIFIED

APPEARANCE

THIN	TRANSLUCENT	SATURATED	OPAQUE

BODY

LIGHT	LIGHT TO MED.	MEDIUM	MED. TO FULL	FULL

SMELL

- ☐ TOAST
- ☐ TOBACCO
- ☐ LEATHER
- ☐ MUSHROOM
- ☐ JAM
- ☐ CHOCOLATE
- ☐ COFFEE
- ☐ SMOKE
- ☐ PEPPER
- ☐ MINT
- ☐ SPICE
- ☐ ALMOND
- ☐ CITRUS
- ☐ MELON
- ☐ OAK
- ☐ BERRIES
- ☐ NUTMEG
- ☐ VEGETAL
- ☐ HONEY
- ☐ APPLE
- ☐ TROPICAL
- ☐ GRASS
- ☐ FLORAL
- ☐ BUTTER
- ☐ ....
- ☐ ....
- ☐ ....
- ☐ ....
- ☐ ....
- ☐ ....

TASTE

- ☐ DARK FRUIT
- ☐ BERRIES
- ☐ PLUMS
- ☐ MUSHROOM
- ☐ TOBACCO
- ☐ CHOCOLATE
- ☐ EARTH
- ☐ PEPPER
- ☐ VANILLA
- ☐ COFFEE
- ☐ LICORICE
- ☐ LEATHER
- ☐ TOAST
- ☐ GRASS
- ☐ CITRUS
- ☐ MELON
- ☐ LYCHEE
- ☐ ALMOND
- ☐ NUTMEG
- ☐ VEGETAL
- ☐ FLORAL
- ☐ HONEY
- ☐ PEARS
- ☐ PEACHES
- ☐ ....
- ☐ ....
- ☐ ....
- ☐ ....
- ☐ ....
- ☐ ....

DRY / SWEETNESS
1	2	3	4	5	6	7	8	9	10

BALANCE
1	2	3	4	5	6	7	8	9	10

TANNINS
1	2	3	4	5	6	7	8	9	10

FLOVOUR INTENSITY
1	2	3	4	5	6	7	8	9	10

FINISH

SHORT	SHORT TO MED.	MEDIUM	MED. TO LONG	LONG

NOTES

PRICE TO VALUE
1	2	3	4	5	6	7	8	9	10

OVERALL RATING
1	2	3	4	5	6	7	8	9	10

WINE _____ **DATE** _____

GRAPE _____ **VINTAGE** _____
PRODUCER _____ **REGION** _____
PRICE _____ **ALCHOOL %** _____

COLOR

| RED | WHITE | ROSE' | SPARKLING | EFFERVESCENT | FORTIFIED |

APPEARANCE

| THIN | TRANSLUCENT | SATURATED | OPAQUE |

BODY

| LIGHT | LIGHT TO MED. | MEDIUM | MED. TO FULL | FULL |

SMELL

- ☐ TOAST
- ☐ TOBACCO
- ☐ LEATHER
- ☐ MUSHROOM
- ☐ JAM
- ☐ CHOCOLATE

- ☐ COFFEE
- ☐ SMOKE
- ☐ PEPPER
- ☐ MINT
- ☐ SPICE
- ☐ ALMOND

- ☐ CITRUS
- ☐ MELON
- ☐ OAK
- ☐ BERRIES
- ☐ NUTMEG
- ☐ VEGETAL

- ☐ HONEY
- ☐ APPLE
- ☐ TROPICAL
- ☐ GRASS
- ☐ FLORAL
- ☐ BUTTER

- ☐ ....
- ☐ ....
- ☐ ....
- ☐ ....
- ☐ ....
- ☐ ....

TASTE

- ☐ DARK FRUIT
- ☐ BERRIES
- ☐ PLUMS
- ☐ MUSHROOM
- ☐ TOBACCO
- ☐ CHOCOLATE

- ☐ EARTH
- ☐ PEPPER
- ☐ VANILLA
- ☐ COFFEE
- ☐ LICORICE
- ☐ LEATHER

- ☐ TOAST
- ☐ GRASS
- ☐ CITRUS
- ☐ MELON
- ☐ LYCHEE
- ☐ ALMOND

- ☐ NUTMEG
- ☐ VEGETAL
- ☐ FLORAL
- ☐ HONEY
- ☐ PEARS
- ☐ PEACHES

- ☐ ....
- ☐ ....
- ☐ ....
- ☐ ....
- ☐ ....
- ☐ ....

DRY / SWEETNESS
| 1 | 2 | 3 | 4 | 5 | 6 | 7 | 8 | 9 | 10 |

BALANCE
| 1 | 2 | 3 | 4 | 5 | 6 | 7 | 8 | 9 | 10 |

TANNINS
| 1 | 2 | 3 | 4 | 5 | 6 | 7 | 8 | 9 | 10 |

FLOVOUR INTENSITY
| 1 | 2 | 3 | 4 | 5 | 6 | 7 | 8 | 9 | 10 |

FINISH

| SHORT | SHORT TO MED. | MEDIUM | MED. TO LONG | LONG |

NOTES

_____
_____
_____
_____
_____

PRICE TO VALUE
| 1 | 2 | 3 | 4 | 5 | 6 | 7 | 8 | 9 | 10 |

OVERALL RATING
| 1 | 2 | 3 | 4 | 5 | 6 | 7 | 8 | 9 | 10 |

WINE		DATE	
GRAPE		**VINTAGE**	
PRODUCER		**REGION**	
PRICE		**ALCHOOL %**	

COLOR

RED	WHITE	ROSE'	SPARKLING	EFFERVESCENT	FORTIFIED

APPEARANCE

THIN	TRANSLUCENT	SATURATED	OPAQUE

BODY

LIGHT	LIGHT TO MED.	MEDIUM	MED. TO FULL	FULL

SMELL

- ☐ TOAST
- ☐ TOBACCO
- ☐ LEATHER
- ☐ MUSHROOM
- ☐ JAM
- ☐ CHOCOLATE
- ☐ COFFEE
- ☐ SMOKE
- ☐ PEPPER
- ☐ MINT
- ☐ SPICE
- ☐ ALMOND
- ☐ CITRUS
- ☐ MELON
- ☐ OAK
- ☐ BERRIES
- ☐ NUTMEG
- ☐ VEGETAL
- ☐ HONEY
- ☐ APPLE
- ☐ TROPICAL
- ☐ GRASS
- ☐ FLORAL
- ☐ BUTTER
- ☐ ....
- ☐ ....
- ☐ ....
- ☐ ....
- ☐ ....
- ☐ ....

TASTE

- ☐ DARK FRUIT
- ☐ BERRIES
- ☐ PLUMS
- ☐ MUSHROOM
- ☐ TOBACCO
- ☐ CHOCOLATE
- ☐ EARTH
- ☐ PEPPER
- ☐ VANILLA
- ☐ COFFEE
- ☐ LICORICE
- ☐ LEATHER
- ☐ TOAST
- ☐ GRASS
- ☐ CITRUS
- ☐ MELON
- ☐ LYCHEE
- ☐ ALMOND
- ☐ NUTMEG
- ☐ VEGETAL
- ☐ FLORAL
- ☐ HONEY
- ☐ PEARS
- ☐ PEACHES
- ☐ ....
- ☐ ....
- ☐ ....
- ☐ ....
- ☐ ....
- ☐ ....

DRY / SWEETNESS

1	2	3	4	5	6	7	8	9	10

BALANCE

1	2	3	4	5	6	7	8	9	10

TANNINS

1	2	3	4	5	6	7	8	9	10

FLOVOUR INTENSITY

1	2	3	4	5	6	7	8	9	10

FINISH

SHORT	SHORT TO MED.	MEDIUM	MED. TO LONG	LONG

NOTES

PRICE TO VALUE

1	2	3	4	5	6	7	8	9	10

OVERALL RATING

1	2	3	4	5	6	7	8	9	10

WINE		DATE	
GRAPE		VINTAGE	
PRODUCER		REGION	
PRICE		ALCHOOL %	

COLOR

RED	WHITE	ROSE'	SPARKLING	EFFERVESCENT	FORTIFIED

APPEARANCE

THIN	TRANSLUCENT	SATURATED	OPAQUE

BODY

LIGHT	LIGHT TO MED.	MEDIUM	MED. TO FULL	FULL

SMELL

- ☐ TOAST
- ☐ TOBACCO
- ☐ LEATHER
- ☐ MUSHROOM
- ☐ JAM
- ☐ CHOCOLATE
- ☐ COFFEE
- ☐ SMOKE
- ☐ PEPPER
- ☐ MINT
- ☐ SPICE
- ☐ ALMOND
- ☐ CITRUS
- ☐ MELON
- ☐ OAK
- ☐ BERRIES
- ☐ NUTMEG
- ☐ VEGETAL
- ☐ HONEY
- ☐ APPLE
- ☐ TROPICAL
- ☐ GRASS
- ☐ FLORAL
- ☐ BUTTER
- ☐ ....
- ☐ ....
- ☐ ....
- ☐ ....
- ☐ ....
- ☐ ....

TASTE

- ☐ DARK FRUIT
- ☐ BERRIES
- ☐ PLUMS
- ☐ MUSHROOM
- ☐ TOBACCO
- ☐ CHOCOLATE
- ☐ EARTH
- ☐ PEPPER
- ☐ VANILLA
- ☐ COFFEE
- ☐ LICORICE
- ☐ LEATHER
- ☐ TOAST
- ☐ GRASS
- ☐ CITRUS
- ☐ MELON
- ☐ LYCHEE
- ☐ ALMOND
- ☐ NUTMEG
- ☐ VEGETAL
- ☐ FLORAL
- ☐ HONEY
- ☐ PEARS
- ☐ PEACHES
- ☐ ....
- ☐ ....
- ☐ ....
- ☐ ....
- ☐ ....
- ☐ ....

DRY / SWEETNESS

1	2	3	4	5	6	7	8	9	10

BALANCE

1	2	3	4	5	6	7	8	9	10

TANNINS

1	2	3	4	5	6	7	8	9	10

FLOVOUR INTENSITY

1	2	3	4	5	6	7	8	9	10

FINISH

SHORT	SHORT TO MED.	MEDIUM	MED. TO LONG	LONG

NOTES

PRICE TO VALUE

1	2	3	4	5	6	7	8	9	10

OVERALL RATING

1	2	3	4	5	6	7	8	9	10

WINE		DATE	
GRAPE		VINTAGE	
PRODUCER		REGION	
PRICE		ALCHOOL %	

COLOR

RED	WHITE	ROSE	SPARKLING	EFFERVESCENT	FORTIFIED

APPEARANCE

THIN	TRANSLUCENT	SATURATED	OPAQUE

BODY

LIGHT	LIGHT TO MED.	MEDIUM	MED. TO FULL	FULL

SMELL

- ☐ TOAST
- ☐ TOBACCO
- ☐ LEATHER
- ☐ MUSHROOM
- ☐ JAM
- ☐ CHOCOLATE
- ☐ COFFEE
- ☐ SMOKE
- ☐ PEPPER
- ☐ MINT
- ☐ SPICE
- ☐ ALMOND
- ☐ CITRUS
- ☐ MELON
- ☐ OAK
- ☐ BERRIES
- ☐ NUTMEG
- ☐ VEGETAL
- ☐ HONEY
- ☐ APPLE
- ☐ TROPICAL
- ☐ GRASS
- ☐ FLORAL
- ☐ BUTTER
- ☐ ....
- ☐ ....
- ☐ ....
- ☐ ....
- ☐ ....
- ☐ ....

TASTE

- ☐ DARK FRUIT
- ☐ BERRIES
- ☐ PLUMS
- ☐ MUSHROOM
- ☐ TOBACCO
- ☐ CHOCOLATE
- ☐ EARTH
- ☐ PEPPER
- ☐ VANILLA
- ☐ COFFEE
- ☐ LICORICE
- ☐ LEATHER
- ☐ TOAST
- ☐ GRASS
- ☐ CITRUS
- ☐ MELON
- ☐ LYCHEE
- ☐ ALMOND
- ☐ NUTMEG
- ☐ VEGETAL
- ☐ FLORAL
- ☐ HONEY
- ☐ PEARS
- ☐ PEACHES
- ☐ ....
- ☐ ....
- ☐ ....
- ☐ ....
- ☐ ....
- ☐ ....

DRY / SWEETNESS

1	2	3	4	5	6	7	8	9	10

BALANCE

1	2	3	4	5	6	7	8	9	10

TANNINS

1	2	3	4	5	6	7	8	9	10

FLOVOUR INTENSITY

1	2	3	4	5	6	7	8	9	10

FINISH

SHORT	SHORT TO MED.	MEDIUM	MED. TO LONG	LONG

NOTES

PRICE TO VALUE

1	2	3	4	5	6	7	8	9	10

OVERALL RATING

1	2	3	4	5	6	7	8	9	10

WINE   **DATE**

GRAPE   **VINTAGE**
PRODUCER   **REGION**
PRICE   **ALCHOOL %**

COLOR

| RED | WHITE | ROSE | SPARKLING | EFFERVESCENT | FORTIFIED |

APPEARANCE

| THIN | TRANSLUCENT | SATURATED | OPAQUE |

BODY

| LIGHT | LIGHT TO MED. | MEDIUM | MED. TO FULL | FULL |

SMELL

- ☐ TOAST
- ☐ TOBACCO
- ☐ LEATHER
- ☐ MUSHROOM
- ☐ JAM
- ☐ CHOCOLATE
- ☐ COFFEE
- ☐ SMOKE
- ☐ PEPPER
- ☐ MINT
- ☐ SPICE
- ☐ ALMOND
- ☐ CITRUS
- ☐ MELON
- ☐ OAK
- ☐ BERRIES
- ☐ NUTMEG
- ☐ VEGETAL
- ☐ HONEY
- ☐ APPLE
- ☐ TROPICAL
- ☐ GRASS
- ☐ FLORAL
- ☐ BUTTER
- ☐ ....
- ☐ ....
- ☐ ....
- ☐ ....
- ☐ ....
- ☐ ....

TASTE

- ☐ DARK FRUIT
- ☐ BERRIES
- ☐ PLUMS
- ☐ MUSHROOM
- ☐ TOBACCO
- ☐ CHOCOLATE
- ☐ EARTH
- ☐ PEPPER
- ☐ VANILLA
- ☐ COFFEE
- ☐ LICORICE
- ☐ LEATHER
- ☐ TOAST
- ☐ GRASS
- ☐ CITRUS
- ☐ MELON
- ☐ LYCHEE
- ☐ ALMOND
- ☐ NUTMEG
- ☐ VEGETAL
- ☐ FLORAL
- ☐ HONEY
- ☐ PEARS
- ☐ PEACHES
- ☐ ....
- ☐ ....
- ☐ ....
- ☐ ....
- ☐ ....
- ☐ ....

DRY / SWEETNESS
| 1 | 2 | 3 | 4 | 5 | 6 | 7 | 8 | 9 | 10 |

BALANCE
| 1 | 2 | 3 | 4 | 5 | 6 | 7 | 8 | 9 | 10 |

TANNINS
| 1 | 2 | 3 | 4 | 5 | 6 | 7 | 8 | 9 | 10 |

FLOVOUR INTENSITY
| 1 | 2 | 3 | 4 | 5 | 6 | 7 | 8 | 9 | 10 |

FINISH
| SHORT | SHORT TO MED. | MEDIUM | MED. TO LONG | LONG |

NOTES

PRICE TO VALUE
| 1 | 2 | 3 | 4 | 5 | 6 | 7 | 8 | 9 | 10 |

OVERALL RATING
| 1 | 2 | 3 | 4 | 5 | 6 | 7 | 8 | 9 | 10 |

WINE _____ **DATE** _____

GRAPE _____ **VINTAGE** _____
PRODUCER _____ **REGION** _____
PRICE _____ **ALCHOOL %** _____

COLOR

| RED | WHITE | ROSE | SPARKLING | EFFERVESCENT | FORTIFIED |

APPEARANCE

| THIN | TRANSLUCENT | SATURATED | OPAQUE |

BODY

| LIGHT | LIGHT TO MED. | MEDIUM | MED. TO FULL | FULL |

SMELL

- ☐ TOAST
- ☐ TOBACCO
- ☐ LEATHER
- ☐ MUSHROOM
- ☐ JAM
- ☐ CHOCOLATE
- ☐ COFFEE
- ☐ SMOKE
- ☐ PEPPER
- ☐ MINT
- ☐ SPICE
- ☐ ALMOND
- ☐ CITRUS
- ☐ MELON
- ☐ OAK
- ☐ BERRIES
- ☐ NUTMEG
- ☐ VEGETAL
- ☐ HONEY
- ☐ APPLE
- ☐ TROPICAL
- ☐ GRASS
- ☐ FLORAL
- ☐ BUTTER
- ☐ ....
- ☐ ....
- ☐ ....
- ☐ ....
- ☐ ....
- ☐ ....

TASTE

- ☐ DARK FRUIT
- ☐ BERRIES
- ☐ PLUMS
- ☐ MUSHROOM
- ☐ TOBACCO
- ☐ CHOCOLATE
- ☐ EARTH
- ☐ PEPPER
- ☐ VANILLA
- ☐ COFFEE
- ☐ LICORICE
- ☐ LEATHER
- ☐ TOAST
- ☐ GRASS
- ☐ CITRUS
- ☐ MELON
- ☐ LYCHEE
- ☐ ALMOND
- ☐ NUTMEG
- ☐ VEGETAL
- ☐ FLORAL
- ☐ HONEY
- ☐ PEARS
- ☐ PEACHES
- ☐ ....
- ☐ ....
- ☐ ....
- ☐ ....
- ☐ ....
- ☐ ....

DRY / SWEETNESS
| 1 | 2 | 3 | 4 | 5 | 6 | 7 | 8 | 9 | 10 |

BALANCE
| 1 | 2 | 3 | 4 | 5 | 6 | 7 | 8 | 9 | 10 |

TANNINS
| 1 | 2 | 3 | 4 | 5 | 6 | 7 | 8 | 9 | 10 |

FLOVOUR INTENSITY
| 1 | 2 | 3 | 4 | 5 | 6 | 7 | 8 | 9 | 10 |

FINISH

| SHORT | SHORT TO MED. | MEDIUM | MED. TO LONG | LONG |

NOTES

_____
_____
_____
_____

PRICE TO VALUE
| 1 | 2 | 3 | 4 | 5 | 6 | 7 | 8 | 9 | 10 |

OVERALL RATING
| 1 | 2 | 3 | 4 | 5 | 6 | 7 | 8 | 9 | 10 |

WINE	DATE
GRAPE	VINTAGE
PRODUCER	REGION
PRICE	ALCHOOL %

COLOR

RED	WHITE	ROSE'	SPARKLING	EFFERVESCENT	FORTIFIED

APPEARANCE

THIN	TRANSLUCENT	SATURATED	OPAQUE

BODY

LIGHT	LIGHT TO MED.	MEDIUM	MED. TO FULL	FULL

SMELL

- ☐ TOAST
- ☐ TOBACCO
- ☐ LEATHER
- ☐ MUSHROOM
- ☐ JAM
- ☐ CHOCOLATE
- ☐ COFFEE
- ☐ SMOKE
- ☐ PEPPER
- ☐ MINT
- ☐ SPICE
- ☐ ALMOND
- ☐ CITRUS
- ☐ MELON
- ☐ OAK
- ☐ BERRIES
- ☐ NUTMEG
- ☐ VEGETAL
- ☐ HONEY
- ☐ APPLE
- ☐ TROPICAL
- ☐ GRASS
- ☐ FLORAL
- ☐ BUTTER
- ☐ ....
- ☐ ....
- ☐ ....
- ☐ ....
- ☐ ....
- ☐ ....

TASTE

- ☐ DARK FRUIT
- ☐ BERRIES
- ☐ PLUMS
- ☐ MUSHROOM
- ☐ TOBACCO
- ☐ CHOCOLATE
- ☐ EARTH
- ☐ PEPPER
- ☐ VANILLA
- ☐ COFFEE
- ☐ LICORICE
- ☐ LEATHER
- ☐ TOAST
- ☐ GRASS
- ☐ CITRUS
- ☐ MELON
- ☐ LYCHEE
- ☐ ALMOND
- ☐ NUTMEG
- ☐ VEGETAL
- ☐ FLORAL
- ☐ HONEY
- ☐ PEARS
- ☐ PEACHES
- ☐ ....
- ☐ ....
- ☐ ....
- ☐ ....
- ☐ ....
- ☐ ....

DRY / SWEETNESS
1	2	3	4	5	6	7	8	9	10

BALANCE
1	2	3	4	5	6	7	8	9	10

TANNINS
1	2	3	4	5	6	7	8	9	10

FLOVOUR INTENSITY
1	2	3	4	5	6	7	8	9	10

FINISH

SHORT	SHORT TO MED.	MEDIUM	MED. TO LONG	LONG

NOTES

PRICE TO VALUE
1	2	3	4	5	6	7	8	9	10

OVERALL RATING
1	2	3	4	5	6	7	8	9	10

WINE _____ **DATE** _____

GRAPE _____ **VINTAGE** _____
PRODUCER _____ **REGION** _____
PRICE _____ **ALCHOOL %** _____

COLOR

| RED | WHITE | ROSE' | SPARKLING | EFFERVESCENT | FORTIFIED |

APPEARANCE

| THIN | TRANSLUCENT | SATURATED | OPAQUE |

BODY

| LIGHT | LIGHT TO MED. | MEDIUM | MED. TO FULL | FULL |

SMELL

- ☐ TOAST
- ☐ TOBACCO
- ☐ LEATHER
- ☐ MUSHROOM
- ☐ JAM
- ☐ CHOCOLATE

- ☐ COFFEE
- ☐ SMOKE
- ☐ PEPPER
- ☐ MINT
- ☐ SPICE
- ☐ ALMOND

- ☐ CITRUS
- ☐ MELON
- ☐ OAK
- ☐ BERRIES
- ☐ NUTMEG
- ☐ VEGETAL

- ☐ HONEY
- ☐ APPLE
- ☐ TROPICAL
- ☐ GRASS
- ☐ FLORAL
- ☐ BUTTER

- ☐ ....
- ☐ ....
- ☐ ....
- ☐ ....
- ☐ ....
- ☐ ....

TASTE

- ☐ DARK FRUIT
- ☐ BERRIES
- ☐ PLUMS
- ☐ MUSHROOM
- ☐ TOBACCO
- ☐ CHOCOLATE

- ☐ EARTH
- ☐ PEPPER
- ☐ VANILLA
- ☐ COFFEE
- ☐ LICORICE
- ☐ LEATHER

- ☐ TOAST
- ☐ GRASS
- ☐ CITRUS
- ☐ MELON
- ☐ LYCHEE
- ☐ ALMOND

- ☐ NUTMEG
- ☐ VEGETAL
- ☐ FLORAL
- ☐ HONEY
- ☐ PEARS
- ☐ PEACHES

- ☐ ....
- ☐ ....
- ☐ ....
- ☐ ....
- ☐ ....
- ☐ ....

DRY / SWEETNESS
| 1 | 2 | 3 | 4 | 5 | 6 | 7 | 8 | 9 | 10 |

BALANCE
| 1 | 2 | 3 | 4 | 5 | 6 | 7 | 8 | 9 | 10 |

TANNINS
| 1 | 2 | 3 | 4 | 5 | 6 | 7 | 8 | 9 | 10 |

FLOVOUR INTENSITY
| 1 | 2 | 3 | 4 | 5 | 6 | 7 | 8 | 9 | 10 |

FINISH

| SHORT | SHORT TO MED. | MEDIUM | MED. TO LONG | LONG |

NOTES

PRICE TO VALUE
| 1 | 2 | 3 | 4 | 5 | 6 | 7 | 8 | 9 | 10 |

OVERALL RATING
| 1 | 2 | 3 | 4 | 5 | 6 | 7 | 8 | 9 | 10 |

WINE		DATE	
GRAPE		VINTAGE	
PRODUCER		REGION	
PRICE		ALCHOOL %	

COLOR

RED	WHITE	ROSE'	SPARKLING	EFFERVESCENT	FORTIFIED

APPEARANCE

THIN	TRANSLUCENT	SATURATED	OPAQUE

BODY

LIGHT	LIGHT TO MED.	MEDIUM	MED. TO FULL	FULL

SMELL

☐ TOAST	☐ COFFEE	☐ CITRUS	☐ HONEY	☐ ....
☐ TOBACCO	☐ SMOKE	☐ MELON	☐ APPLE	☐ ....
☐ LEATHER	☐ PEPPER	☐ OAK	☐ TROPICAL	☐ ....
☐ MUSHROOM	☐ MINT	☐ BERRIES	☐ GRASS	☐ ....
☐ JAM	☐ SPICE	☐ NUTMEG	☐ FLORAL	☐ ....
☐ CHOCOLATE	☐ ALMOND	☐ VEGETAL	☐ BUTTER	☐ ....

TASTE

☐ DARK FRUIT	☐ EARTH	☐ TOAST	☐ NUTMEG	☐ ....
☐ BERRIES	☐ PEPPER	☐ GRASS	☐ VEGETAL	☐ ....
☐ PLUMS	☐ VANILLA	☐ CITRUS	☐ FLORAL	☐ ....
☐ MUSHROOM	☐ COFFEE	☐ MELON	☐ HONEY	☐ ....
☐ TOBACCO	☐ LICORICE	☐ LYCHEE	☐ PEARS	☐ ....
☐ CHOCOLATE	☐ LEATHER	☐ ALMOND	☐ PEACHES	☐ ....

DRY / SWEETNESS

1	2	3	4	5	6	7	8	9	10

BALANCE

1	2	3	4	5	6	7	8	9	10

TANNINS

1	2	3	4	5	6	7	8	9	10

FLOVOUR INTENSITY

1	2	3	4	5	6	7	8	9	10

FINISH

SHORT	SHORT TO MED.	MEDIUM	MED. TO LONG	LONG

NOTES

PRICE TO VALUE

1	2	3	4	5	6	7	8	9	10

OVERALL RATING

1	2	3	4	5	6	7	8	9	10

WINE _____ **DATE** _____

GRAPE _____ **VINTAGE** _____
PRODUCER _____ **REGION** _____
PRICE _____ **ALCHOOL %** _____

COLOR
| RED | WHITE | ROSE | SPARKLING | EFFERVESCENT | FORTIFIED |

APPEARANCE
| THIN | TRANSLUCENT | SATURATED | OPAQUE |

BODY
| LIGHT | LIGHT TO MED. | MEDIUM | MED. TO FULL | FULL |

SMELL
- ☐ TOAST
- ☐ TOBACCO
- ☐ LEATHER
- ☐ MUSHROOM
- ☐ JAM
- ☐ CHOCOLATE
- ☐ COFFEE
- ☐ SMOKE
- ☐ PEPPER
- ☐ MINT
- ☐ SPICE
- ☐ ALMOND
- ☐ CITRUS
- ☐ MELON
- ☐ OAK
- ☐ BERRIES
- ☐ NUTMEG
- ☐ VEGETAL
- ☐ HONEY
- ☐ APPLE
- ☐ TROPICAL
- ☐ GRASS
- ☐ FLORAL
- ☐ BUTTER
- ☐ ....
- ☐ ....
- ☐ ....
- ☐ ....
- ☐ ....
- ☐ ....

TASTE
- ☐ DARK FRUIT
- ☐ BERRIES
- ☐ PLUMS
- ☐ MUSHROOM
- ☐ TOBACCO
- ☐ CHOCOLATE
- ☐ EARTH
- ☐ PEPPER
- ☐ VANILLA
- ☐ COFFEE
- ☐ LICORICE
- ☐ LEATHER
- ☐ TOAST
- ☐ GRASS
- ☐ CITRUS
- ☐ MELON
- ☐ LYCHEE
- ☐ ALMOND
- ☐ NUTMEG
- ☐ VEGETAL
- ☐ FLORAL
- ☐ HONEY
- ☐ PEARS
- ☐ PEACHES
- ☐ ....
- ☐ ....
- ☐ ....
- ☐ ....
- ☐ ....
- ☐ ....

DRY / SWEETNESS
| 1 | 2 | 3 | 4 | 5 | 6 | 7 | 8 | 9 | 10 |

BALANCE
| 1 | 2 | 3 | 4 | 5 | 6 | 7 | 8 | 9 | 10 |

TANNINS
| 1 | 2 | 3 | 4 | 5 | 6 | 7 | 8 | 9 | 10 |

FLOVOUR INTENSITY
| 1 | 2 | 3 | 4 | 5 | 6 | 7 | 8 | 9 | 10 |

FINISH
| SHORT | SHORT TO MED. | MEDIUM | MED. TO LONG | LONG |

NOTES
_____
_____
_____
_____
_____

PRICE TO VALUE
| 1 | 2 | 3 | 4 | 5 | 6 | 7 | 8 | 9 | 10 |

OVERALL RATING
| 1 | 2 | 3 | 4 | 5 | 6 | 7 | 8 | 9 | 10 |

WINE _____ **DATE** _____

GRAPE _____ **VINTAGE** _____
PRODUCER _____ **REGION** _____
PRICE _____ **ALCHOOL %** _____

COLOR

| RED | WHITE | ROSE' | SPARKLING | EFFERVESCENT | FORTIFIED |

APPEARANCE

| THIN | TRANSLUCENT | SATURATED | OPAQUE |

BODY

| LIGHT | LIGHT TO MED. | MEDIUM | MED. TO FULL | FULL |

SMELL

- ☐ TOAST
- ☐ TOBACCO
- ☐ LEATHER
- ☐ MUSHROOM
- ☐ JAM
- ☐ CHOCOLATE

- ☐ COFFEE
- ☐ SMOKE
- ☐ PEPPER
- ☐ MINT
- ☐ SPICE
- ☐ ALMOND

- ☐ CITRUS
- ☐ MELON
- ☐ OAK
- ☐ BERRIES
- ☐ NUTMEG
- ☐ VEGETAL

- ☐ HONEY
- ☐ APPLE
- ☐ TROPICAL
- ☐ GRASS
- ☐ FLORAL
- ☐ BUTTER

- ☐ ....
- ☐ ....
- ☐ ....
- ☐ ....
- ☐ ....
- ☐ ....

TASTE

- ☐ DARK FRUIT
- ☐ BERRIES
- ☐ PLUMS
- ☐ MUSHROOM
- ☐ TOBACCO
- ☐ CHOCOLATE

- ☐ EARTH
- ☐ PEPPER
- ☐ VANILLA
- ☐ COFFEE
- ☐ LICORICE
- ☐ LEATHER

- ☐ TOAST
- ☐ GRASS
- ☐ CITRUS
- ☐ MELON
- ☐ LYCHEE
- ☐ ALMOND

- ☐ NUTMEG
- ☐ VEGETAL
- ☐ FLORAL
- ☐ HONEY
- ☐ PEARS
- ☐ PEACHES

- ☐ ....
- ☐ ....
- ☐ ....
- ☐ ....
- ☐ ....
- ☐ ....

DRY / SWEETNESS
| 1 | 2 | 3 | 4 | 5 | 6 | 7 | 8 | 9 | 10 |

BALANCE
| 1 | 2 | 3 | 4 | 5 | 6 | 7 | 8 | 9 | 10 |

TANNINS
| 1 | 2 | 3 | 4 | 5 | 6 | 7 | 8 | 9 | 10 |

FLOVOUR INTENSITY
| 1 | 2 | 3 | 4 | 5 | 6 | 7 | 8 | 9 | 10 |

FINISH

| SHORT | SHORT TO MED. | MEDIUM | MED. TO LONG | LONG |

NOTES

_____
_____
_____
_____
_____
_____

PRICE TO VALUE
| 1 | 2 | 3 | 4 | 5 | 6 | 7 | 8 | 9 | 10 |

OVERALL RATING
| 1 | 2 | 3 | 4 | 5 | 6 | 7 | 8 | 9 | 10 |

WINE _____   **DATE** _____

GRAPE _____   **VINTAGE** _____
PRODUCER _____   **REGION** _____
PRICE _____   **ALCHOOL %** _____

COLOR

| RED | WHITE | ROSE' | SPARKLING | EFFERVESCENT | FORTIFIED |

APPEARANCE

| THIN | TRANSLUCENT | SATURATED | OPAQUE |

BODY

| LIGHT | LIGHT TO MED. | MEDIUM | MED. TO FULL | FULL |

SMELL

- ☐ TOAST
- ☐ TOBACCO
- ☐ LEATHER
- ☐ MUSHROOM
- ☐ JAM
- ☐ CHOCOLATE
- ☐ COFFEE
- ☐ SMOKE
- ☐ PEPPER
- ☐ MINT
- ☐ SPICE
- ☐ ALMOND
- ☐ CITRUS
- ☐ MELON
- ☐ OAK
- ☐ BERRIES
- ☐ NUTMEG
- ☐ VEGETAL
- ☐ HONEY
- ☐ APPLE
- ☐ TROPICAL
- ☐ GRASS
- ☐ FLORAL
- ☐ BUTTER
- ☐ ....
- ☐ ....
- ☐ ....
- ☐ ....
- ☐ ....
- ☐ ....

TASTE

- ☐ DARK FRUIT
- ☐ BERRIES
- ☐ PLUMS
- ☐ MUSHROOM
- ☐ TOBACCO
- ☐ CHOCOLATE
- ☐ EARTH
- ☐ PEPPER
- ☐ VANILLA
- ☐ COFFEE
- ☐ LICORICE
- ☐ LEATHER
- ☐ TOAST
- ☐ GRASS
- ☐ CITRUS
- ☐ MELON
- ☐ LYCHEE
- ☐ ALMOND
- ☐ NUTMEG
- ☐ VEGETAL
- ☐ FLORAL
- ☐ HONEY
- ☐ PEARS
- ☐ PEACHES
- ☐ ....
- ☐ ....
- ☐ ....
- ☐ ....
- ☐ ....
- ☐ ....

DRY / SWEETNESS
| 1 | 2 | 3 | 4 | 5 | 6 | 7 | 8 | 9 | 10 |

BALANCE
| 1 | 2 | 3 | 4 | 5 | 6 | 7 | 8 | 9 | 10 |

TANNINS
| 1 | 2 | 3 | 4 | 5 | 6 | 7 | 8 | 9 | 10 |

FLOVOUR INTENSITY
| 1 | 2 | 3 | 4 | 5 | 6 | 7 | 8 | 9 | 10 |

FINISH

| SHORT | SHORT TO MED. | MEDIUM | MED. TO LONG | LONG |

NOTES

PRICE TO VALUE
| 1 | 2 | 3 | 4 | 5 | 6 | 7 | 8 | 9 | 10 |

OVERALL RATING
| 1 | 2 | 3 | 4 | 5 | 6 | 7 | 8 | 9 | 10 |

WINE _____ **DATE** _____

GRAPE _____ **VINTAGE** _____
PRODUCER _____ **REGION** _____
PRICE _____ **ALCHOOL %** _____

COLOR

| RED | WHITE | ROSE' | SPARKLING | EFFERVESCENT | FORTIFIED |

APPEARANCE

| THIN | TRANSLUCENT | SATURATED | OPAQUE |

BODY

| LIGHT | LIGHT TO MED. | MEDIUM | MED. TO FULL | FULL |

SMELL

- ☐ TOAST
- ☐ TOBACCO
- ☐ LEATHER
- ☐ MUSHROOM
- ☐ JAM
- ☐ CHOCOLATE
- ☐ COFFEE
- ☐ SMOKE
- ☐ PEPPER
- ☐ MINT
- ☐ SPICE
- ☐ ALMOND
- ☐ CITRUS
- ☐ MELON
- ☐ OAK
- ☐ BERRIES
- ☐ NUTMEG
- ☐ VEGETAL
- ☐ HONEY
- ☐ APPLE
- ☐ TROPICAL
- ☐ GRASS
- ☐ FLORAL
- ☐ BUTTER
- ☐ ....
- ☐ ....
- ☐ ....
- ☐ ....
- ☐ ....
- ☐ ....

TASTE

- ☐ DARK FRUIT
- ☐ BERRIES
- ☐ PLUMS
- ☐ MUSHROOM
- ☐ TOBACCO
- ☐ CHOCOLATE
- ☐ EARTH
- ☐ PEPPER
- ☐ VANILLA
- ☐ COFFEE
- ☐ LICORICE
- ☐ LEATHER
- ☐ TOAST
- ☐ GRASS
- ☐ CITRUS
- ☐ MELON
- ☐ LYCHEE
- ☐ ALMOND
- ☐ NUTMEG
- ☐ VEGETAL
- ☐ FLORAL
- ☐ HONEY
- ☐ PEARS
- ☐ PEACHES
- ☐ ....
- ☐ ....
- ☐ ....
- ☐ ....
- ☐ ....
- ☐ ....

DRY / SWEETNESS
| 1 | 2 | 3 | 4 | 5 | 6 | 7 | 8 | 9 | 10 |

BALANCE
| 1 | 2 | 3 | 4 | 5 | 6 | 7 | 8 | 9 | 10 |

TANNINS
| 1 | 2 | 3 | 4 | 5 | 6 | 7 | 8 | 9 | 10 |

FLOVOUR INTENSITY
| 1 | 2 | 3 | 4 | 5 | 6 | 7 | 8 | 9 | 10 |

FINISH
| SHORT | SHORT TO MED. | MEDIUM | MED. TO LONG | LONG |

NOTES

PRICE TO VALUE
| 1 | 2 | 3 | 4 | 5 | 6 | 7 | 8 | 9 | 10 |

OVERALL RATING
| 1 | 2 | 3 | 4 | 5 | 6 | 7 | 8 | 9 | 10 |

WINE		DATE	
GRAPE		**VINTAGE**	
PRODUCER		**REGION**	
PRICE		**ALCHOOL %**	

COLOR

RED	WHITE	ROSE'	SPARKLING	EFFERVESCENT	FORTIFIED

APPEARANCE

THIN	TRANSLUCENT	SATURATED	OPAQUE

BODY

LIGHT	LIGHT TO MED.	MEDIUM	MED. TO FULL	FULL

SMELL

- ☐ TOAST
- ☐ TOBACCO
- ☐ LEATHER
- ☐ MUSHROOM
- ☐ JAM
- ☐ CHOCOLATE
- ☐ COFFEE
- ☐ SMOKE
- ☐ PEPPER
- ☐ MINT
- ☐ SPICE
- ☐ ALMOND
- ☐ CITRUS
- ☐ MELON
- ☐ OAK
- ☐ BERRIES
- ☐ NUTMEG
- ☐ VEGETAL
- ☐ HONEY
- ☐ APPLE
- ☐ TROPICAL
- ☐ GRASS
- ☐ FLORAL
- ☐ BUTTER
- ☐ ....
- ☐ ....
- ☐ ....
- ☐ ....
- ☐ ....
- ☐ ....

TASTE

- ☐ DARK FRUIT
- ☐ BERRIES
- ☐ PLUMS
- ☐ MUSHROOM
- ☐ TOBACCO
- ☐ CHOCOLATE
- ☐ EARTH
- ☐ PEPPER
- ☐ VANILLA
- ☐ COFFEE
- ☐ LICORICE
- ☐ LEATHER
- ☐ TOAST
- ☐ GRASS
- ☐ CITRUS
- ☐ MELON
- ☐ LYCHEE
- ☐ ALMOND
- ☐ NUTMEG
- ☐ VEGETAL
- ☐ FLORAL
- ☐ HONEY
- ☐ PEARS
- ☐ PEACHES
- ☐ ....
- ☐ ....
- ☐ ....
- ☐ ....
- ☐ ....
- ☐ ....

DRY / SWEETNESS

1	2	3	4	5	6	7	8	9	10

BALANCE

1	2	3	4	5	6	7	8	9	10

TANNINS

1	2	3	4	5	6	7	8	9	10

FLOVOUR INTENSITY

1	2	3	4	5	6	7	8	9	10

FINISH

SHORT	SHORT TO MED.	MEDIUM	MED. TO LONG	LONG

NOTES

PRICE TO VALUE

1	2	3	4	5	6	7	8	9	10

OVERALL RATING

1	2	3	4	5	6	7	8	9	10

WINE _____   **DATE** _____

GRAPE _____   **VINTAGE** _____
PRODUCER _____   **REGION** _____
PRICE _____   **ALCHOOL %** _____

COLOR

RED	WHITE	ROSE'	SPARKLING	EFFERVESCENT	FORTIFIED

APPEARANCE

THIN	TRANSLUCENT	SATURATED	OPAQUE

BODY

LIGHT	LIGHT TO MED.	MEDIUM	MED. TO FULL	FULL

SMELL

- ☐ TOAST
- ☐ TOBACCO
- ☐ LEATHER
- ☐ MUSHROOM
- ☐ JAM
- ☐ CHOCOLATE
- ☐ COFFEE
- ☐ SMOKE
- ☐ PEPPER
- ☐ MINT
- ☐ SPICE
- ☐ ALMOND
- ☐ CITRUS
- ☐ MELON
- ☐ OAK
- ☐ BERRIES
- ☐ NUTMEG
- ☐ VEGETAL
- ☐ HONEY
- ☐ APPLE
- ☐ TROPICAL
- ☐ GRASS
- ☐ FLORAL
- ☐ BUTTER
- ☐ ....
- ☐ ....
- ☐ ....
- ☐ ....
- ☐ ....
- ☐ ....

TASTE

- ☐ DARK FRUIT
- ☐ BERRIES
- ☐ PLUMS
- ☐ MUSHROOM
- ☐ TOBACCO
- ☐ CHOCOLATE
- ☐ EARTH
- ☐ PEPPER
- ☐ VANILLA
- ☐ COFFEE
- ☐ LICORICE
- ☐ LEATHER
- ☐ TOAST
- ☐ GRASS
- ☐ CITRUS
- ☐ MELON
- ☐ LYCHEE
- ☐ ALMOND
- ☐ NUTMEG
- ☐ VEGETAL
- ☐ FLORAL
- ☐ HONEY
- ☐ PEARS
- ☐ PEACHES
- ☐ ....
- ☐ ....
- ☐ ....
- ☐ ....
- ☐ ....
- ☐ ....

DRY / SWEETNESS

1	2	3	4	5	6	7	8	9	10

BALANCE

1	2	3	4	5	6	7	8	9	10

TANNINS

1	2	3	4	5	6	7	8	9	10

FLOVOUR INTENSITY

1	2	3	4	5	6	7	8	9	10

FINISH

SHORT	SHORT TO MED.	MEDIUM	MED. TO LONG	LONG

NOTES

PRICE TO VALUE

1	2	3	4	5	6	7	8	9	10

OVERALL RATING

1	2	3	4	5	6	7	8	9	10

WINE		DATE	
GRAPE		VINTAGE	
PRODUCER		REGION	
PRICE		ALCHOOL %	

COLOR

RED	WHITE	ROSE	SPARKLING	EFFERVESCENT	FORTIFIED

APPEARANCE

THIN	TRANSLUCENT	SATURATED	OPAQUE

BODY

LIGHT	LIGHT TO MED.	MEDIUM	MED. TO FULL	FULL

SMELL

- ☐ TOAST
- ☐ TOBACCO
- ☐ LEATHER
- ☐ MUSHROOM
- ☐ JAM
- ☐ CHOCOLATE
- ☐ COFFEE
- ☐ SMOKE
- ☐ PEPPER
- ☐ MINT
- ☐ SPICE
- ☐ ALMOND
- ☐ CITRUS
- ☐ MELON
- ☐ OAK
- ☐ BERRIES
- ☐ NUTMEG
- ☐ VEGETAL
- ☐ HONEY
- ☐ APPLE
- ☐ TROPICAL
- ☐ GRASS
- ☐ FLORAL
- ☐ BUTTER
- ☐ ....
- ☐ ....
- ☐ ....
- ☐ ....
- ☐ ....
- ☐ ....

TASTE

- ☐ DARK FRUIT
- ☐ BERRIES
- ☐ PLUMS
- ☐ MUSHROOM
- ☐ TOBACCO
- ☐ CHOCOLATE
- ☐ EARTH
- ☐ PEPPER
- ☐ VANILLA
- ☐ COFFEE
- ☐ LICORICE
- ☐ LEATHER
- ☐ TOAST
- ☐ GRASS
- ☐ CITRUS
- ☐ MELON
- ☐ LYCHEE
- ☐ ALMOND
- ☐ NUTMEG
- ☐ VEGETAL
- ☐ FLORAL
- ☐ HONEY
- ☐ PEARS
- ☐ PEACHES
- ☐ ....
- ☐ ....
- ☐ ....
- ☐ ....
- ☐ ....
- ☐ ....

DRY / SWEETNESS

1	2	3	4	5	6	7	8	9	10

BALANCE

1	2	3	4	5	6	7	8	9	10

TANNINS

1	2	3	4	5	6	7	8	9	10

FLOVOUR INTENSITY

1	2	3	4	5	6	7	8	9	10

FINISH

SHORT	SHORT TO MED.	MEDIUM	MED. TO LONG	LONG

NOTES

PRICE TO VALUE

1	2	3	4	5	6	7	8	9	10

OVERALL RATING

1	2	3	4	5	6	7	8	9	10

WINE _____ **DATE** _____

GRAPE _____ **VINTAGE** _____
PRODUCER _____ **REGION** _____
PRICE _____ **ALCHOOL %** _____

COLOR

| RED | WHITE | ROSE | SPARKLING | EFFERVESCENT | FORTIFIED |

APPEARANCE

| THIN | TRANSLUCENT | SATURATED | OPAQUE |

BODY

| LIGHT | LIGHT TO MED. | MEDIUM | MED. TO FULL | FULL |

SMELL

- ☐ TOAST
- ☐ TOBACCO
- ☐ LEATHER
- ☐ MUSHROOM
- ☐ JAM
- ☐ CHOCOLATE

- ☐ COFFEE
- ☐ SMOKE
- ☐ PEPPER
- ☐ MINT
- ☐ SPICE
- ☐ ALMOND

- ☐ CITRUS
- ☐ MELON
- ☐ OAK
- ☐ BERRIES
- ☐ NUTMEG
- ☐ VEGETAL

- ☐ HONEY
- ☐ APPLE
- ☐ TROPICAL
- ☐ GRASS
- ☐ FLORAL
- ☐ BUTTER

- ☐ ....
- ☐ ....
- ☐ ....
- ☐ ....
- ☐ ....
- ☐ ....

TASTE

- ☐ DARK FRUIT
- ☐ BERRIES
- ☐ PLUMS
- ☐ MUSHROOM
- ☐ TOBACCO
- ☐ CHOCOLATE

- ☐ EARTH
- ☐ PEPPER
- ☐ VANILLA
- ☐ COFFEE
- ☐ LICORICE
- ☐ LEATHER

- ☐ TOAST
- ☐ GRASS
- ☐ CITRUS
- ☐ MELON
- ☐ LYCHEE
- ☐ ALMOND

- ☐ NUTMEG
- ☐ VEGETAL
- ☐ FLORAL
- ☐ HONEY
- ☐ PEARS
- ☐ PEACHES

- ☐ ....
- ☐ ....
- ☐ ....
- ☐ ....
- ☐ ....
- ☐ ....

DRY / SWEETNESS
| 1 | 2 | 3 | 4 | 5 | 6 | 7 | 8 | 9 | 10 |

BALANCE
| 1 | 2 | 3 | 4 | 5 | 6 | 7 | 8 | 9 | 10 |

TANNINS
| 1 | 2 | 3 | 4 | 5 | 6 | 7 | 8 | 9 | 10 |

FLOVOUR INTENSITY
| 1 | 2 | 3 | 4 | 5 | 6 | 7 | 8 | 9 | 10 |

FINISH

| SHORT | SHORT TO MED. | MEDIUM | MED. TO LONG | LONG |

NOTES

_____
_____
_____
_____
_____

PRICE TO VALUE
| 1 | 2 | 3 | 4 | 5 | 6 | 7 | 8 | 9 | 10 |

OVERALL RATING
| 1 | 2 | 3 | 4 | 5 | 6 | 7 | 8 | 9 | 10 |

WINE		DATE	
GRAPE		VINTAGE	
PRODUCER		REGION	
PRICE		ALCHOOL %	

COLOR

RED	WHITE	ROSE'	SPARKLING	EFFERVESCENT	FORTIFIED

APPEARANCE

THIN	TRANSLUCENT	SATURATED	OPAQUE

BODY

LIGHT	LIGHT TO MED.	MEDIUM	MED. TO FULL	FULL

SMELL

- ☐ TOAST
- ☐ TOBACCO
- ☐ LEATHER
- ☐ MUSHROOM
- ☐ JAM
- ☐ CHOCOLATE
- ☐ COFFEE
- ☐ SMOKE
- ☐ PEPPER
- ☐ MINT
- ☐ SPICE
- ☐ ALMOND
- ☐ CITRUS
- ☐ MELON
- ☐ OAK
- ☐ BERRIES
- ☐ NUTMEG
- ☐ VEGETAL
- ☐ HONEY
- ☐ APPLE
- ☐ TROPICAL
- ☐ GRASS
- ☐ FLORAL
- ☐ BUTTER
- ☐ ....
- ☐ ....
- ☐ ....
- ☐ ....
- ☐ ....
- ☐ ....

TASTE

- ☐ DARK FRUIT
- ☐ BERRIES
- ☐ PLUMS
- ☐ MUSHROOM
- ☐ TOBACCO
- ☐ CHOCOLATE
- ☐ EARTH
- ☐ PEPPER
- ☐ VANILLA
- ☐ COFFEE
- ☐ LICORICE
- ☐ LEATHER
- ☐ TOAST
- ☐ GRASS
- ☐ CITRUS
- ☐ MELON
- ☐ LYCHEE
- ☐ ALMOND
- ☐ NUTMEG
- ☐ VEGETAL
- ☐ FLORAL
- ☐ HONEY
- ☐ PEARS
- ☐ PEACHES
- ☐ ....
- ☐ ....
- ☐ ....
- ☐ ....
- ☐ ....
- ☐ ....

DRY / SWEETNESS

1	2	3	4	5	6	7	8	9	10

BALANCE

1	2	3	4	5	6	7	8	9	10

TANNINS

1	2	3	4	5	6	7	8	9	10

FLOVOUR INTENSITY

1	2	3	4	5	6	7	8	9	10

FINISH

SHORT	SHORT TO MED.	MEDIUM	MED. TO LONG	LONG

NOTES

PRICE TO VALUE

1	2	3	4	5	6	7	8	9	10

OVERALL RATING

1	2	3	4	5	6	7	8	9	10

WINE _____   **DATE** _____

GRAPE _____   **VINTAGE** _____
PRODUCER _____   **REGION** _____
PRICE _____   **ALCHOOL %** _____

COLOR

RED	WHITE	ROSE'	SPARKLING	EFFERVESCENT	FORTIFIED

APPEARANCE

THIN	TRANSLUCENT	SATURATED	OPAQUE

BODY

LIGHT	LIGHT TO MED.	MEDIUM	MED. TO FULL	FULL

SMELL

- ☐ TOAST
- ☐ TOBACCO
- ☐ LEATHER
- ☐ MUSHROOM
- ☐ JAM
- ☐ CHOCOLATE
- ☐ COFFEE
- ☐ SMOKE
- ☐ PEPPER
- ☐ MINT
- ☐ SPICE
- ☐ ALMOND
- ☐ CITRUS
- ☐ MELON
- ☐ OAK
- ☐ BERRIES
- ☐ NUTMEG
- ☐ VEGETAL
- ☐ HONEY
- ☐ APPLE
- ☐ TROPICAL
- ☐ GRASS
- ☐ FLORAL
- ☐ BUTTER
- ☐ ....
- ☐ ....
- ☐ ....
- ☐ ....
- ☐ ....
- ☐ ....

TASTE

- ☐ DARK FRUIT
- ☐ BERRIES
- ☐ PLUMS
- ☐ MUSHROOM
- ☐ TOBACCO
- ☐ CHOCOLATE
- ☐ EARTH
- ☐ PEPPER
- ☐ VANILLA
- ☐ COFFEE
- ☐ LICORICE
- ☐ LEATHER
- ☐ TOAST
- ☐ GRASS
- ☐ CITRUS
- ☐ MELON
- ☐ LYCHEE
- ☐ ALMOND
- ☐ NUTMEG
- ☐ VEGETAL
- ☐ FLORAL
- ☐ HONEY
- ☐ PEARS
- ☐ PEACHES
- ☐ ....
- ☐ ....
- ☐ ....
- ☐ ....
- ☐ ....
- ☐ ....

DRY / SWEETNESS

1	2	3	4	5	6	7	8	9	10

BALANCE

1	2	3	4	5	6	7	8	9	10

TANNINS

1	2	3	4	5	6	7	8	9	10

FLOVOUR INTENSITY

1	2	3	4	5	6	7	8	9	10

FINISH

SHORT	SHORT TO MED.	MEDIUM	MED. TO LONG	LONG

NOTES

_____
_____
_____
_____
_____

PRICE TO VALUE

1	2	3	4	5	6	7	8	9	10

OVERALL RATING

1	2	3	4	5	6	7	8	9	10

WINE _____   **DATE** _____

GRAPE _____   **VINTAGE** _____
PRODUCER _____   **REGION** _____
PRICE _____   **ALCHOOL %** _____

COLOR

| RED | WHITE | ROSE' | SPARKLING | EFFERVESCENT | FORTIFIED |

APPEARANCE

| THIN | TRANSLUCENT | SATURATED | OPAQUE |

BODY

| LIGHT | LIGHT TO MED. | MEDIUM | MED. TO FULL | FULL |

SMELL

- ☐ TOAST
- ☐ TOBACCO
- ☐ LEATHER
- ☐ MUSHROOM
- ☐ JAM
- ☐ CHOCOLATE
- ☐ COFFEE
- ☐ SMOKE
- ☐ PEPPER
- ☐ MINT
- ☐ SPICE
- ☐ ALMOND
- ☐ CITRUS
- ☐ MELON
- ☐ OAK
- ☐ BERRIES
- ☐ NUTMEG
- ☐ VEGETAL
- ☐ HONEY
- ☐ APPLE
- ☐ TROPICAL
- ☐ GRASS
- ☐ FLORAL
- ☐ BUTTER
- ☐ ....
- ☐ ....
- ☐ ....
- ☐ ....
- ☐ ....
- ☐ ....

TASTE

- ☐ DARK FRUIT
- ☐ BERRIES
- ☐ PLUMS
- ☐ MUSHROOM
- ☐ TOBACCO
- ☐ CHOCOLATE
- ☐ EARTH
- ☐ PEPPER
- ☐ VANILLA
- ☐ COFFEE
- ☐ LICORICE
- ☐ LEATHER
- ☐ TOAST
- ☐ GRASS
- ☐ CITRUS
- ☐ MELON
- ☐ LYCHEE
- ☐ ALMOND
- ☐ NUTMEG
- ☐ VEGETAL
- ☐ FLORAL
- ☐ HONEY
- ☐ PEARS
- ☐ PEACHES
- ☐ ....
- ☐ ....
- ☐ ....
- ☐ ....
- ☐ ....
- ☐ ....

DRY / SWEETNESS
| 1 | 2 | 3 | 4 | 5 | 6 | 7 | 8 | 9 | 10 |

BALANCE
| 1 | 2 | 3 | 4 | 5 | 6 | 7 | 8 | 9 | 10 |

TANNINS
| 1 | 2 | 3 | 4 | 5 | 6 | 7 | 8 | 9 | 10 |

FLOVOUR INTENSITY
| 1 | 2 | 3 | 4 | 5 | 6 | 7 | 8 | 9 | 10 |

FINISH

| SHORT | SHORT TO MED. | MEDIUM | MED. TO LONG | LONG |

NOTES
_____
_____
_____
_____
_____

PRICE TO VALUE
| 1 | 2 | 3 | 4 | 5 | 6 | 7 | 8 | 9 | 10 |

OVERALL RATING
| 1 | 2 | 3 | 4 | 5 | 6 | 7 | 8 | 9 | 10 |

WINE _____ **DATE** _____

GRAPE _____ **VINTAGE** _____
PRODUCER _____ **REGION** _____
PRICE _____ **ALCHOOL %** _____

COLOR

| RED | WHITE | ROSE' | SPARKLING | EFFERVESCENT | FORTIFIED |

APPEARANCE

| THIN | TRANSLUCENT | SATURATED | OPAQUE |

BODY

| LIGHT | LIGHT TO MED. | MEDIUM | MED. TO FULL | FULL |

SMELL

- ☐ TOAST
- ☐ TOBACCO
- ☐ LEATHER
- ☐ MUSHROOM
- ☐ JAM
- ☐ CHOCOLATE
- ☐ COFFEE
- ☐ SMOKE
- ☐ PEPPER
- ☐ MINT
- ☐ SPICE
- ☐ ALMOND
- ☐ CITRUS
- ☐ MELON
- ☐ OAK
- ☐ BERRIES
- ☐ NUTMEG
- ☐ VEGETAL
- ☐ HONEY
- ☐ APPLE
- ☐ TROPICAL
- ☐ GRASS
- ☐ FLORAL
- ☐ BUTTER
- ☐ ....
- ☐ ....
- ☐ ....
- ☐ ....
- ☐ ....
- ☐ ....

TASTE

- ☐ DARK FRUIT
- ☐ BERRIES
- ☐ PLUMS
- ☐ MUSHROOM
- ☐ TOBACCO
- ☐ CHOCOLATE
- ☐ EARTH
- ☐ PEPPER
- ☐ VANILLA
- ☐ COFFEE
- ☐ LICORICE
- ☐ LEATHER
- ☐ TOAST
- ☐ GRASS
- ☐ CITRUS
- ☐ MELON
- ☐ LYCHEE
- ☐ ALMOND
- ☐ NUTMEG
- ☐ VEGETAL
- ☐ FLORAL
- ☐ HONEY
- ☐ PEARS
- ☐ PEACHES
- ☐ ....
- ☐ ....
- ☐ ....
- ☐ ....
- ☐ ....
- ☐ ....

DRY / SWEETNESS
| 1 | 2 | 3 | 4 | 5 | 6 | 7 | 8 | 9 | 10 |

BALANCE
| 1 | 2 | 3 | 4 | 5 | 6 | 7 | 8 | 9 | 10 |

TANNINS
| 1 | 2 | 3 | 4 | 5 | 6 | 7 | 8 | 9 | 10 |

FLOVOUR INTENSITY
| 1 | 2 | 3 | 4 | 5 | 6 | 7 | 8 | 9 | 10 |

FINISH

| SHORT | SHORT TO MED. | MEDIUM | MED. TO LONG | LONG |

NOTES

PRICE TO VALUE
| 1 | 2 | 3 | 4 | 5 | 6 | 7 | 8 | 9 | 10 |

OVERALL RATING
| 1 | 2 | 3 | 4 | 5 | 6 | 7 | 8 | 9 | 10 |

WINE   **DATE**

GRAPE   **VINTAGE**
PRODUCER   **REGION**
PRICE   **ALCHOOL %**

COLOR

RED	WHITE	ROSE	SPARKLING	EFFERVESCENT	FORTIFIED

APPEARANCE

THIN	TRANSLUCENT	SATURATED	OPAQUE

BODY

LIGHT	LIGHT TO MED.	MEDIUM	MED. TO FULL	FULL

SMELL

- ☐ TOAST
- ☐ TOBACCO
- ☐ LEATHER
- ☐ MUSHROOM
- ☐ JAM
- ☐ CHOCOLATE
- ☐ COFFEE
- ☐ SMOKE
- ☐ PEPPER
- ☐ MINT
- ☐ SPICE
- ☐ ALMOND
- ☐ CITRUS
- ☐ MELON
- ☐ OAK
- ☐ BERRIES
- ☐ NUTMEG
- ☐ VEGETAL
- ☐ HONEY
- ☐ APPLE
- ☐ TROPICAL
- ☐ GRASS
- ☐ FLORAL
- ☐ BUTTER
- ☐ ....
- ☐ ....
- ☐ ....
- ☐ ....
- ☐ ....
- ☐ ....

TASTE

- ☐ DARK FRUIT
- ☐ BERRIES
- ☐ PLUMS
- ☐ MUSHROOM
- ☐ TOBACCO
- ☐ CHOCOLATE
- ☐ EARTH
- ☐ PEPPER
- ☐ VANILLA
- ☐ COFFEE
- ☐ LICORICE
- ☐ LEATHER
- ☐ TOAST
- ☐ GRASS
- ☐ CITRUS
- ☐ MELON
- ☐ LYCHEE
- ☐ ALMOND
- ☐ NUTMEG
- ☐ VEGETAL
- ☐ FLORAL
- ☐ HONEY
- ☐ PEARS
- ☐ PEACHES
- ☐ ....
- ☐ ....
- ☐ ....
- ☐ ....
- ☐ ....
- ☐ ....

DRY / SWEETNESS

1	2	3	4	5	6	7	8	9	10

BALANCE

1	2	3	4	5	6	7	8	9	10

TANNINS

1	2	3	4	5	6	7	8	9	10

FLOVOUR INTENSITY

1	2	3	4	5	6	7	8	9	10

FINISH

SHORT	SHORT TO MED.	MEDIUM	MED. TO LONG	LONG

NOTES

PRICE TO VALUE

1	2	3	4	5	6	7	8	9	10

OVERALL RATING

1	2	3	4	5	6	7	8	9	10

WINE _____ **DATE** _____

GRAPE _____ **VINTAGE** _____
PRODUCER _____ **REGION** _____
PRICE _____ **ALCHOOL %** _____

COLOR

RED	WHITE	ROSE	SPARKLING	EFFERVESCENT	FORTIFIED

APPEARANCE

THIN	TRANSLUCENT	SATURATED	OPAQUE

BODY

LIGHT	LIGHT TO MED.	MEDIUM	MED. TO FULL	FULL

SMELL

- ☐ TOAST
- ☐ TOBACCO
- ☐ LEATHER
- ☐ MUSHROOM
- ☐ JAM
- ☐ CHOCOLATE
- ☐ COFFEE
- ☐ SMOKE
- ☐ PEPPER
- ☐ MINT
- ☐ SPICE
- ☐ ALMOND
- ☐ CITRUS
- ☐ MELON
- ☐ OAK
- ☐ BERRIES
- ☐ NUTMEG
- ☐ VEGETAL
- ☐ HONEY
- ☐ APPLE
- ☐ TROPICAL
- ☐ GRASS
- ☐ FLORAL
- ☐ BUTTER
- ☐ ....
- ☐ ....
- ☐ ....
- ☐ ....
- ☐ ....
- ☐ ....

TASTE

- ☐ DARK FRUIT
- ☐ BERRIES
- ☐ PLUMS
- ☐ MUSHROOM
- ☐ TOBACCO
- ☐ CHOCOLATE
- ☐ EARTH
- ☐ PEPPER
- ☐ VANILLA
- ☐ COFFEE
- ☐ LICORICE
- ☐ LEATHER
- ☐ TOAST
- ☐ GRASS
- ☐ CITRUS
- ☐ MELON
- ☐ LYCHEE
- ☐ ALMOND
- ☐ NUTMEG
- ☐ VEGETAL
- ☐ FLORAL
- ☐ HONEY
- ☐ PEARS
- ☐ PEACHES
- ☐ ....
- ☐ ....
- ☐ ....
- ☐ ....
- ☐ ....
- ☐ ....

DRY / SWEETNESS
1	2	3	4	5	6	7	8	9	10

BALANCE
1	2	3	4	5	6	7	8	9	10

TANNINS
1	2	3	4	5	6	7	8	9	10

FLOVOUR INTENSITY
1	2	3	4	5	6	7	8	9	10

FINISH

SHORT	SHORT TO MED.	MEDIUM	MED. TO LONG	LONG

NOTES

PRICE TO VALUE
1	2	3	4	5	6	7	8	9	10

OVERALL RATING
1	2	3	4	5	6	7	8	9	10

WINE		DATE	
GRAPE		VINTAGE	
PRODUCER		REGION	
PRICE		ALCHOOL %	

COLOR

RED	WHITE	ROSE	SPARKLING	EFFERVESCENT	FORTIFIED

APPEARANCE

THIN	TRANSLUCENT	SATURATED	OPAQUE

BODY

LIGHT	LIGHT TO MED.	MEDIUM	MED. TO FULL	FULL

SMELL

☐ TOAST	☐ COFFEE	☐ CITRUS	☐ HONEY	☐ ....
☐ TOBACCO	☐ SMOKE	☐ MELON	☐ APPLE	☐ ....
☐ LEATHER	☐ PEPPER	☐ OAK	☐ TROPICAL	☐ ....
☐ MUSHROOM	☐ MINT	☐ BERRIES	☐ GRASS	☐ ....
☐ JAM	☐ SPICE	☐ NUTMEG	☐ FLORAL	☐ ....
☐ CHOCOLATE	☐ ALMOND	☐ VEGETAL	☐ BUTTER	☐ ....

TASTE

☐ DARK FRUIT	☐ EARTH	☐ TOAST	☐ NUTMEG	☐ ....
☐ BERRIES	☐ PEPPER	☐ GRASS	☐ VEGETAL	☐ ....
☐ PLUMS	☐ VANILLA	☐ CITRUS	☐ FLORAL	☐ ....
☐ MUSHROOM	☐ COFFEE	☐ MELON	☐ HONEY	☐ ....
☐ TOBACCO	☐ LICORICE	☐ LYCHEE	☐ PEARS	☐ ....
☐ CHOCOLATE	☐ LEATHER	☐ ALMOND	☐ PEACHES	☐ ....

DRY / SWEETNESS
1	2	3	4	5	6	7	8	9	10

BALANCE
1	2	3	4	5	6	7	8	9	10

TANNINS
1	2	3	4	5	6	7	8	9	10

FLOVOUR INTENSITY
1	2	3	4	5	6	7	8	9	10

FINISH

SHORT	SHORT TO MED.	MEDIUM	MED. TO LONG	LONG

NOTES

PRICE TO VALUE
1	2	3	4	5	6	7	8	9	10

OVERALL RATING
1	2	3	4	5	6	7	8	9	10

WINE   **DATE**

GRAPE   **VINTAGE**
PRODUCER   **REGION**
PRICE   **ALCHOOL %**

COLOR

| RED | WHITE | ROSE' | SPARKLING | EFFERVESCENT | FORTIFIED |

APPEARANCE

| THIN | TRANSLUCENT | SATURATED | OPAQUE |

BODY

| LIGHT | LIGHT TO MED. | MEDIUM | MED. TO FULL | FULL |

SMELL

- ☐ TOAST
- ☐ TOBACCO
- ☐ LEATHER
- ☐ MUSHROOM
- ☐ JAM
- ☐ CHOCOLATE
- ☐ COFFEE
- ☐ SMOKE
- ☐ PEPPER
- ☐ MINT
- ☐ SPICE
- ☐ ALMOND
- ☐ CITRUS
- ☐ MELON
- ☐ OAK
- ☐ BERRIES
- ☐ NUTMEG
- ☐ VEGETAL
- ☐ HONEY
- ☐ APPLE
- ☐ TROPICAL
- ☐ GRASS
- ☐ FLORAL
- ☐ BUTTER
- ☐ ....
- ☐ ....
- ☐ ....
- ☐ ....
- ☐ ....
- ☐ ....

TASTE

- ☐ DARK FRUIT
- ☐ BERRIES
- ☐ PLUMS
- ☐ MUSHROOM
- ☐ TOBACCO
- ☐ CHOCOLATE
- ☐ EARTH
- ☐ PEPPER
- ☐ VANILLA
- ☐ COFFEE
- ☐ LICORICE
- ☐ LEATHER
- ☐ TOAST
- ☐ GRASS
- ☐ CITRUS
- ☐ MELON
- ☐ LYCHEE
- ☐ ALMOND
- ☐ NUTMEG
- ☐ VEGETAL
- ☐ FLORAL
- ☐ HONEY
- ☐ PEARS
- ☐ PEACHES
- ☐ ....
- ☐ ....
- ☐ ....
- ☐ ....
- ☐ ....
- ☐ ....

DRY / SWEETNESS
| 1 | 2 | 3 | 4 | 5 | 6 | 7 | 8 | 9 | 10 |

BALANCE
| 1 | 2 | 3 | 4 | 5 | 6 | 7 | 8 | 9 | 10 |

TANNINS
| 1 | 2 | 3 | 4 | 5 | 6 | 7 | 8 | 9 | 10 |

FLOVOUR INTENSITY
| 1 | 2 | 3 | 4 | 5 | 6 | 7 | 8 | 9 | 10 |

FINISH

| SHORT | SHORT TO MED. | MEDIUM | MED. TO LONG | LONG |

NOTES

PRICE TO VALUE
| 1 | 2 | 3 | 4 | 5 | 6 | 7 | 8 | 9 | 10 |

OVERALL RATING
| 1 | 2 | 3 | 4 | 5 | 6 | 7 | 8 | 9 | 10 |

WINE   **DATE**

GRAPE   **VINTAGE**
PRODUCER   **REGION**
PRICE   **ALCHOOL %**

COLOR

RED	WHITE	ROSE'	SPARKLING	EFFERVESCENT	FORTIFIED

APPEARANCE

THIN	TRANSLUCENT	SATURATED	OPAQUE

BODY

LIGHT	LIGHT TO MED.	MEDIUM	MED. TO FULL	FULL

SMELL

☐ TOAST	☐ COFFEE	☐ CITRUS	☐ HONEY	☐ ....
☐ TOBACCO	☐ SMOKE	☐ MELON	☐ APPLE	☐ ....
☐ LEATHER	☐ PEPPER	☐ OAK	☐ TROPICAL	☐ ....
☐ MUSHROOM	☐ MINT	☐ BERRIES	☐ GRASS	☐ ....
☐ JAM	☐ SPICE	☐ NUTMEG	☐ FLORAL	☐ ....
☐ CHOCOLATE	☐ ALMOND	☐ VEGETAL	☐ BUTTER	☐ ....

TASTE

☐ DARK FRUIT	☐ EARTH	☐ TOAST	☐ NUTMEG	☐ ....
☐ BERRIES	☐ PEPPER	☐ GRASS	☐ VEGETAL	☐ ....
☐ PLUMS	☐ VANILLA	☐ CITRUS	☐ FLORAL	☐ ....
☐ MUSHROOM	☐ COFFEE	☐ MELON	☐ HONEY	☐ ....
☐ TOBACCO	☐ LICORICE	☐ LYCHEE	☐ PEARS	☐ ....
☐ CHOCOLATE	☐ LEATHER	☐ ALMOND	☐ PEACHES	☐ ....

DRY / SWEETNESS
1	2	3	4	5	6	7	8	9	10

BALANCE
1	2	3	4	5	6	7	8	9	10

TANNINS
1	2	3	4	5	6	7	8	9	10

FLOVOUR INTENSITY
1	2	3	4	5	6	7	8	9	10

FINISH

SHORT	SHORT TO MED.	MEDIUM	MED. TO LONG	LONG

NOTES

PRICE TO VALUE
1	2	3	4	5	6	7	8	9	10

OVERALL RATING
1	2	3	4	5	6	7	8	9	10

WINE _____ **DATE** _____

GRAPE _____ **VINTAGE** _____
PRODUCER _____ **REGION** _____
PRICE _____ **ALCHOOL %** _____

COLOR

| RED | WHITE | ROSE' | SPARKLING | EFFERVESCENT | FORTIFIED |

APPEARANCE

| THIN | TRANSLUCENT | SATURATED | OPAQUE |

BODY

| LIGHT | LIGHT TO MED. | MEDIUM | MED. TO FULL | FULL |

SMELL

- ☐ TOAST
- ☐ TOBACCO
- ☐ LEATHER
- ☐ MUSHROOM
- ☐ JAM
- ☐ CHOCOLATE
- ☐ COFFEE
- ☐ SMOKE
- ☐ PEPPER
- ☐ MINT
- ☐ SPICE
- ☐ ALMOND
- ☐ CITRUS
- ☐ MELON
- ☐ OAK
- ☐ BERRIES
- ☐ NUTMEG
- ☐ VEGETAL
- ☐ HONEY
- ☐ APPLE
- ☐ TROPICAL
- ☐ GRASS
- ☐ FLORAL
- ☐ BUTTER
- ☐ ....
- ☐ ....
- ☐ ....
- ☐ ....
- ☐ ....
- ☐ ....

TASTE

- ☐ DARK FRUIT
- ☐ BERRIES
- ☐ PLUMS
- ☐ MUSHROOM
- ☐ TOBACCO
- ☐ CHOCOLATE
- ☐ EARTH
- ☐ PEPPER
- ☐ VANILLA
- ☐ COFFEE
- ☐ LICORICE
- ☐ LEATHER
- ☐ TOAST
- ☐ GRASS
- ☐ CITRUS
- ☐ MELON
- ☐ LYCHEE
- ☐ ALMOND
- ☐ NUTMEG
- ☐ VEGETAL
- ☐ FLORAL
- ☐ HONEY
- ☐ PEARS
- ☐ PEACHES
- ☐ ....
- ☐ ....
- ☐ ....
- ☐ ....
- ☐ ....
- ☐ ....

DRY / SWEETNESS
| 1 | 2 | 3 | 4 | 5 | 6 | 7 | 8 | 9 | 10 |

BALANCE
| 1 | 2 | 3 | 4 | 5 | 6 | 7 | 8 | 9 | 10 |

TANNINS
| 1 | 2 | 3 | 4 | 5 | 6 | 7 | 8 | 9 | 10 |

FLOVOUR INTENSITY
| 1 | 2 | 3 | 4 | 5 | 6 | 7 | 8 | 9 | 10 |

FINISH

| SHORT | SHORT TO MED. | MEDIUM | MED. TO LONG | LONG |

NOTES

PRICE TO VALUE
| 1 | 2 | 3 | 4 | 5 | 6 | 7 | 8 | 9 | 10 |

OVERALL RATING
| 1 | 2 | 3 | 4 | 5 | 6 | 7 | 8 | 9 | 10 |

WINE _____   **DATE** _____

GRAPE _____   **VINTAGE** _____
PRODUCER _____   **REGION** _____
PRICE _____   **ALCHOOL %** _____

COLOR

RED	WHITE	ROSE'	SPARKLING	EFFERVESCENT	FORTIFIED

APPEARANCE

THIN	TRANSLUCENT	SATURATED	OPAQUE

BODY

LIGHT	LIGHT TO MED.	MEDIUM	MED. TO FULL	FULL

SMELL

- ☐ TOAST
- ☐ TOBACCO
- ☐ LEATHER
- ☐ MUSHROOM
- ☐ JAM
- ☐ CHOCOLATE
- ☐ COFFEE
- ☐ SMOKE
- ☐ PEPPER
- ☐ MINT
- ☐ SPICE
- ☐ ALMOND
- ☐ CITRUS
- ☐ MELON
- ☐ OAK
- ☐ BERRIES
- ☐ NUTMEG
- ☐ VEGETAL
- ☐ HONEY
- ☐ APPLE
- ☐ TROPICAL
- ☐ GRASS
- ☐ FLORAL
- ☐ BUTTER
- ☐ ....
- ☐ ....
- ☐ ....
- ☐ ....
- ☐ ....
- ☐ ....

TASTE

- ☐ DARK FRUIT
- ☐ BERRIES
- ☐ PLUMS
- ☐ MUSHROOM
- ☐ TOBACCO
- ☐ CHOCOLATE
- ☐ EARTH
- ☐ PEPPER
- ☐ VANILLA
- ☐ COFFEE
- ☐ LICORICE
- ☐ LEATHER
- ☐ TOAST
- ☐ GRASS
- ☐ CITRUS
- ☐ MELON
- ☐ LYCHEE
- ☐ ALMOND
- ☐ NUTMEG
- ☐ VEGETAL
- ☐ FLORAL
- ☐ HONEY
- ☐ PEARS
- ☐ PEACHES
- ☐ ....
- ☐ ....
- ☐ ....
- ☐ ....
- ☐ ....
- ☐ ....

DRY / SWEETNESS

1	2	3	4	5	6	7	8	9	10

BALANCE

1	2	3	4	5	6	7	8	9	10

TANNINS

1	2	3	4	5	6	7	8	9	10

FLOVOUR INTENSITY

1	2	3	4	5	6	7	8	9	10

FINISH

SHORT	SHORT TO MED.	MEDIUM	MED. TO LONG	LONG

NOTES

_____
_____
_____
_____
_____

PRICE TO VALUE

1	2	3	4	5	6	7	8	9	10

OVERALL RATING

1	2	3	4	5	6	7	8	9	10

WINE _____ **DATE** _____

GRAPE _____ **VINTAGE** _____
PRODUCER _____ **REGION** _____
PRICE _____ **ALCHOOL %** _____

COLOR

RED	WHITE	ROSE	SPARKLING	EFFERVESCENT	FORTIFIED

APPEARANCE

THIN	TRANSLUCENT	SATURATED	OPAQUE

BODY

LIGHT	LIGHT TO MED.	MEDIUM	MED. TO FULL	FULL

SMELL

- ☐ TOAST
- ☐ TOBACCO
- ☐ LEATHER
- ☐ MUSHROOM
- ☐ JAM
- ☐ CHOCOLATE
- ☐ COFFEE
- ☐ SMOKE
- ☐ PEPPER
- ☐ MINT
- ☐ SPICE
- ☐ ALMOND
- ☐ CITRUS
- ☐ MELON
- ☐ OAK
- ☐ BERRIES
- ☐ NUTMEG
- ☐ VEGETAL
- ☐ HONEY
- ☐ APPLE
- ☐ TROPICAL
- ☐ GRASS
- ☐ FLORAL
- ☐ BUTTER
- ☐ ....
- ☐ ....
- ☐ ....
- ☐ ....
- ☐ ....
- ☐ ....

TASTE

- ☐ DARK FRUIT
- ☐ BERRIES
- ☐ PLUMS
- ☐ MUSHROOM
- ☐ TOBACCO
- ☐ CHOCOLATE
- ☐ EARTH
- ☐ PEPPER
- ☐ VANILLA
- ☐ COFFEE
- ☐ LICORICE
- ☐ LEATHER
- ☐ TOAST
- ☐ GRASS
- ☐ CITRUS
- ☐ MELON
- ☐ LYCHEE
- ☐ ALMOND
- ☐ NUTMEG
- ☐ VEGETAL
- ☐ FLORAL
- ☐ HONEY
- ☐ PEARS
- ☐ PEACHES
- ☐ ....
- ☐ ....
- ☐ ....
- ☐ ....
- ☐ ....
- ☐ ....

DRY / SWEETNESS
1	2	3	4	5	6	7	8	9	10

BALANCE
1	2	3	4	5	6	7	8	9	10

TANNINS
1	2	3	4	5	6	7	8	9	10

FLOVOUR INTENSITY
1	2	3	4	5	6	7	8	9	10

FINISH

SHORT	SHORT TO MED.	MEDIUM	MED. TO LONG	LONG

NOTES
_____
_____
_____
_____
_____

PRICE TO VALUE
1	2	3	4	5	6	7	8	9	10

OVERALL RATING
1	2	3	4	5	6	7	8	9	10

WINE		DATE	
GRAPE		VINTAGE	
PRODUCER		REGION	
PRICE		ALCHOOL %	

COLOR

RED	WHITE	ROSE	SPARKLING	EFFERVESCENT	FORTIFIED

APPEARANCE

THIN	TRANSLUCENT	SATURATED	OPAQUE

BODY

LIGHT	LIGHT TO MED.	MEDIUM	MED. TO FULL	FULL

SMELL

- ☐ TOAST
- ☐ TOBACCO
- ☐ LEATHER
- ☐ MUSHROOM
- ☐ JAM
- ☐ CHOCOLATE
- ☐ COFFEE
- ☐ SMOKE
- ☐ PEPPER
- ☐ MINT
- ☐ SPICE
- ☐ ALMOND
- ☐ CITRUS
- ☐ MELON
- ☐ OAK
- ☐ BERRIES
- ☐ NUTMEG
- ☐ VEGETAL
- ☐ HONEY
- ☐ APPLE
- ☐ TROPICAL
- ☐ GRASS
- ☐ FLORAL
- ☐ BUTTER
- ☐ ....
- ☐ ....
- ☐ ....
- ☐ ....
- ☐ ....
- ☐ ....

TASTE

- ☐ DARK FRUIT
- ☐ BERRIES
- ☐ PLUMS
- ☐ MUSHROOM
- ☐ TOBACCO
- ☐ CHOCOLATE
- ☐ EARTH
- ☐ PEPPER
- ☐ VANILLA
- ☐ COFFEE
- ☐ LICORICE
- ☐ LEATHER
- ☐ TOAST
- ☐ GRASS
- ☐ CITRUS
- ☐ MELON
- ☐ LYCHEE
- ☐ ALMOND
- ☐ NUTMEG
- ☐ VEGETAL
- ☐ FLORAL
- ☐ HONEY
- ☐ PEARS
- ☐ PEACHES
- ☐ ....
- ☐ ....
- ☐ ....
- ☐ ....
- ☐ ....
- ☐ ....

DRY / SWEETNESS
1	2	3	4	5	6	7	8	9	10

BALANCE
1	2	3	4	5	6	7	8	9	10

TANNINS
1	2	3	4	5	6	7	8	9	10

FLOVOUR INTENSITY
1	2	3	4	5	6	7	8	9	10

FINISH

SHORT	SHORT TO MED.	MEDIUM	MED. TO LONG	LONG

NOTES

PRICE TO VALUE
1	2	3	4	5	6	7	8	9	10

OVERALL RATING
1	2	3	4	5	6	7	8	9	10

WINE   **DATE**

GRAPE   **VINTAGE**
PRODUCER   **REGION**
PRICE   **ALCHOOL %**

COLOR

RED	WHITE	ROSE'	SPARKLING	EFFERVESCENT	FORTIFIED

APPEARANCE

THIN	TRANSLUCENT	SATURATED	OPAQUE

BODY

LIGHT	LIGHT TO MED.	MEDIUM	MED. TO FULL	FULL

SMELL

- ☐ TOAST
- ☐ TOBACCO
- ☐ LEATHER
- ☐ MUSHROOM
- ☐ JAM
- ☐ CHOCOLATE
- ☐ COFFEE
- ☐ SMOKE
- ☐ PEPPER
- ☐ MINT
- ☐ SPICE
- ☐ ALMOND
- ☐ CITRUS
- ☐ MELON
- ☐ OAK
- ☐ BERRIES
- ☐ NUTMEG
- ☐ VEGETAL
- ☐ HONEY
- ☐ APPLE
- ☐ TROPICAL
- ☐ GRASS
- ☐ FLORAL
- ☐ BUTTER
- ☐ ....
- ☐ ....
- ☐ ....
- ☐ ....
- ☐ ....
- ☐ ....

TASTE

- ☐ DARK FRUIT
- ☐ BERRIES
- ☐ PLUMS
- ☐ MUSHROOM
- ☐ TOBACCO
- ☐ CHOCOLATE
- ☐ EARTH
- ☐ PEPPER
- ☐ VANILLA
- ☐ COFFEE
- ☐ LICORICE
- ☐ LEATHER
- ☐ TOAST
- ☐ GRASS
- ☐ CITRUS
- ☐ MELON
- ☐ LYCHEE
- ☐ ALMOND
- ☐ NUTMEG
- ☐ VEGETAL
- ☐ FLORAL
- ☐ HONEY
- ☐ PEARS
- ☐ PEACHES
- ☐ ....
- ☐ ....
- ☐ ....
- ☐ ....
- ☐ ....
- ☐ ....

DRY / SWEETNESS

1	2	3	4	5	6	7	8	9	10

BALANCE

1	2	3	4	5	6	7	8	9	10

TANNINS

1	2	3	4	5	6	7	8	9	10

FLOVOUR INTENSITY

1	2	3	4	5	6	7	8	9	10

FINISH

SHORT	SHORT TO MED.	MEDIUM	MED. TO LONG	LONG

NOTES

PRICE TO VALUE

1	2	3	4	5	6	7	8	9	10

OVERALL RATING

1	2	3	4	5	6	7	8	9	10

WINE _____ **DATE** _____

GRAPE _____ **VINTAGE** _____
PRODUCER _____ **REGION** _____
PRICE _____ **ALCHOOL %** _____

COLOR

RED	WHITE	ROSE'	SPARKLING	EFFERVESCENT	FORTIFIED

APPEARANCE

THIN	TRANSLUCENT	SATURATED	OPAQUE

BODY

LIGHT	LIGHT TO MED.	MEDIUM	MED. TO FULL	FULL

SMELL

- ☐ TOAST
- ☐ TOBACCO
- ☐ LEATHER
- ☐ MUSHROOM
- ☐ JAM
- ☐ CHOCOLATE
- ☐ COFFEE
- ☐ SMOKE
- ☐ PEPPER
- ☐ MINT
- ☐ SPICE
- ☐ ALMOND
- ☐ CITRUS
- ☐ MELON
- ☐ OAK
- ☐ BERRIES
- ☐ NUTMEG
- ☐ VEGETAL
- ☐ HONEY
- ☐ APPLE
- ☐ TROPICAL
- ☐ GRASS
- ☐ FLORAL
- ☐ BUTTER
- ☐ ....
- ☐ ....
- ☐ ....
- ☐ ....
- ☐ ....
- ☐ ....

TASTE

- ☐ DARK FRUIT
- ☐ BERRIES
- ☐ PLUMS
- ☐ MUSHROOM
- ☐ TOBACCO
- ☐ CHOCOLATE
- ☐ EARTH
- ☐ PEPPER
- ☐ VANILLA
- ☐ COFFEE
- ☐ LICORICE
- ☐ LEATHER
- ☐ TOAST
- ☐ GRASS
- ☐ CITRUS
- ☐ MELON
- ☐ LYCHEE
- ☐ ALMOND
- ☐ NUTMEG
- ☐ VEGETAL
- ☐ FLORAL
- ☐ HONEY
- ☐ PEARS
- ☐ PEACHES
- ☐ ....
- ☐ ....
- ☐ ....
- ☐ ....
- ☐ ....
- ☐ ....

DRY / SWEETNESS

1	2	3	4	5	6	7	8	9	10

BALANCE

1	2	3	4	5	6	7	8	9	10

TANNINS

1	2	3	4	5	6	7	8	9	10

FLOVOUR INTENSITY

1	2	3	4	5	6	7	8	9	10

FINISH

SHORT	SHORT TO MED.	MEDIUM	MED. TO LONG	LONG

NOTES

_____
_____
_____
_____
_____

PRICE TO VALUE

1	2	3	4	5	6	7	8	9	10

OVERALL RATING

1	2	3	4	5	6	7	8	9	10

WINE		DATE	
GRAPE		VINTAGE	
PRODUCER		REGION	
PRICE		ALCHOOL %	

COLOR

RED	WHITE	ROSE'	SPARKLING	EFFERVESCENT	FORTIFIED

APPEARANCE

THIN	TRANSLUCENT	SATURATED	OPAQUE

BODY

LIGHT	LIGHT TO MED.	MEDIUM	MED. TO FULL	FULL

SMELL

- ☐ TOAST
- ☐ TOBACCO
- ☐ LEATHER
- ☐ MUSHROOM
- ☐ JAM
- ☐ CHOCOLATE
- ☐ COFFEE
- ☐ SMOKE
- ☐ PEPPER
- ☐ MINT
- ☐ SPICE
- ☐ ALMOND
- ☐ CITRUS
- ☐ MELON
- ☐ OAK
- ☐ BERRIES
- ☐ NUTMEG
- ☐ VEGETAL
- ☐ HONEY
- ☐ APPLE
- ☐ TROPICAL
- ☐ GRASS
- ☐ FLORAL
- ☐ BUTTER
- ☐ ....
- ☐ ....
- ☐ ....
- ☐ ....
- ☐ ....
- ☐ ....

TASTE

- ☐ DARK FRUIT
- ☐ BERRIES
- ☐ PLUMS
- ☐ MUSHROOM
- ☐ TOBACCO
- ☐ CHOCOLATE
- ☐ EARTH
- ☐ PEPPER
- ☐ VANILLA
- ☐ COFFEE
- ☐ LICORICE
- ☐ LEATHER
- ☐ TOAST
- ☐ GRASS
- ☐ CITRUS
- ☐ MELON
- ☐ LYCHEE
- ☐ ALMOND
- ☐ NUTMEG
- ☐ VEGETAL
- ☐ FLORAL
- ☐ HONEY
- ☐ PEARS
- ☐ PEACHES
- ☐ ....
- ☐ ....
- ☐ ....
- ☐ ....
- ☐ ....
- ☐ ....

DRY / SWEETNESS
1	2	3	4	5	6	7	8	9	10

BALANCE
1	2	3	4	5	6	7	8	9	10

TANNINS
1	2	3	4	5	6	7	8	9	10

FLOVOUR INTENSITY
1	2	3	4	5	6	7	8	9	10

FINISH

SHORT	SHORT TO MED.	MEDIUM	MED. TO LONG	LONG

NOTES

PRICE TO VALUE
1	2	3	4	5	6	7	8	9	10

OVERALL RATING
1	2	3	4	5	6	7	8	9	10

WINE _____ **DATE** _____

GRAPE _____ **VINTAGE** _____
PRODUCER _____ **REGION** _____
PRICE _____ **ALCHOOL %** _____

COLOR

RED	WHITE	ROSE	SPARKLING	EFFERVESCENT	FORTIFIED

APPEARANCE

THIN	TRANSLUCENT	SATURATED	OPAQUE

BODY

LIGHT	LIGHT TO MED.	MEDIUM	MED. TO FULL	FULL

SMELL

- ☐ TOAST
- ☐ TOBACCO
- ☐ LEATHER
- ☐ MUSHROOM
- ☐ JAM
- ☐ CHOCOLATE
- ☐ COFFEE
- ☐ SMOKE
- ☐ PEPPER
- ☐ MINT
- ☐ SPICE
- ☐ ALMOND
- ☐ CITRUS
- ☐ MELON
- ☐ OAK
- ☐ BERRIES
- ☐ NUTMEG
- ☐ VEGETAL
- ☐ HONEY
- ☐ APPLE
- ☐ TROPICAL
- ☐ GRASS
- ☐ FLORAL
- ☐ BUTTER
- ☐ ....
- ☐ ....
- ☐ ....
- ☐ ....
- ☐ ....
- ☐ ....

TASTE

- ☐ DARK FRUIT
- ☐ BERRIES
- ☐ PLUMS
- ☐ MUSHROOM
- ☐ TOBACCO
- ☐ CHOCOLATE
- ☐ EARTH
- ☐ PEPPER
- ☐ VANILLA
- ☐ COFFEE
- ☐ LICORICE
- ☐ LEATHER
- ☐ TOAST
- ☐ GRASS
- ☐ CITRUS
- ☐ MELON
- ☐ LYCHEE
- ☐ ALMOND
- ☐ NUTMEG
- ☐ VEGETAL
- ☐ FLORAL
- ☐ HONEY
- ☐ PEARS
- ☐ PEACHES
- ☐ ....
- ☐ ....
- ☐ ....
- ☐ ....
- ☐ ....
- ☐ ....

DRY / SWEETNESS

1	2	3	4	5	6	7	8	9	10

BALANCE

1	2	3	4	5	6	7	8	9	10

TANNINS

1	2	3	4	5	6	7	8	9	10

FLOVOUR INTENSITY

1	2	3	4	5	6	7	8	9	10

FINISH

SHORT	SHORT TO MED.	MEDIUM	MED. TO LONG	LONG

NOTES

_____
_____
_____
_____

PRICE TO VALUE

1	2	3	4	5	6	7	8	9	10

OVERALL RATING

1	2	3	4	5	6	7	8	9	10

WINE		DATE	
GRAPE		VINTAGE	
PRODUCER		REGION	
PRICE		ALCHOOL %	

COLOR

RED	WHITE	ROSE	SPARKLING	EFFERVESCENT	FORTIFIED

APPEARANCE

THIN	TRANSLUCENT	SATURATED	OPAQUE

BODY

LIGHT	LIGHT TO MED.	MEDIUM	MED. TO FULL	FULL

SMELL

- ☐ TOAST
- ☐ TOBACCO
- ☐ LEATHER
- ☐ MUSHROOM
- ☐ JAM
- ☐ CHOCOLATE
- ☐ COFFEE
- ☐ SMOKE
- ☐ PEPPER
- ☐ MINT
- ☐ SPICE
- ☐ ALMOND
- ☐ CITRUS
- ☐ MELON
- ☐ OAK
- ☐ BERRIES
- ☐ NUTMEG
- ☐ VEGETAL
- ☐ HONEY
- ☐ APPLE
- ☐ TROPICAL
- ☐ GRASS
- ☐ FLORAL
- ☐ BUTTER
- ☐ ....
- ☐ ....
- ☐ ....
- ☐ ....
- ☐ ....
- ☐ ....

TASTE

- ☐ DARK FRUIT
- ☐ BERRIES
- ☐ PLUMS
- ☐ MUSHROOM
- ☐ TOBACCO
- ☐ CHOCOLATE
- ☐ EARTH
- ☐ PEPPER
- ☐ VANILLA
- ☐ COFFEE
- ☐ LICORICE
- ☐ LEATHER
- ☐ TOAST
- ☐ GRASS
- ☐ CITRUS
- ☐ MELON
- ☐ LYCHEE
- ☐ ALMOND
- ☐ NUTMEG
- ☐ VEGETAL
- ☐ FLORAL
- ☐ HONEY
- ☐ PEARS
- ☐ PEACHES
- ☐ ....
- ☐ ....
- ☐ ....
- ☐ ....
- ☐ ....
- ☐ ....

DRY / SWEETNESS

1	2	3	4	5	6	7	8	9	10

BALANCE

1	2	3	4	5	6	7	8	9	10

TANNINS

1	2	3	4	5	6	7	8	9	10

FLOVOUR INTENSITY

1	2	3	4	5	6	7	8	9	10

FINISH

SHORT	SHORT TO MED.	MEDIUM	MED. TO LONG	LONG

NOTES

PRICE TO VALUE

1	2	3	4	5	6	7	8	9	10

OVERALL RATING

1	2	3	4	5	6	7	8	9	10

WINE _____   **DATE** _____

GRAPE _____   **VINTAGE** _____
PRODUCER _____   **REGION** _____
PRICE _____   **ALCHOOL %** _____

COLOR

RED	WHITE	ROSE'	SPARKLING	EFFERVESCENT	FORTIFIED

APPEARANCE

THIN	TRANSLUCENT	SATURATED	OPAQUE

BODY

LIGHT	LIGHT TO MED.	MEDIUM	MED. TO FULL	FULL

SMELL

- ☐ TOAST
- ☐ TOBACCO
- ☐ LEATHER
- ☐ MUSHROOM
- ☐ JAM
- ☐ CHOCOLATE
- ☐ COFFEE
- ☐ SMOKE
- ☐ PEPPER
- ☐ MINT
- ☐ SPICE
- ☐ ALMOND
- ☐ CITRUS
- ☐ MELON
- ☐ OAK
- ☐ BERRIES
- ☐ NUTMEG
- ☐ VEGETAL
- ☐ HONEY
- ☐ APPLE
- ☐ TROPICAL
- ☐ GRASS
- ☐ FLORAL
- ☐ BUTTER
- ☐ ....
- ☐ ....
- ☐ ....
- ☐ ....
- ☐ ....
- ☐ ....

TASTE

- ☐ DARK FRUIT
- ☐ BERRIES
- ☐ PLUMS
- ☐ MUSHROOM
- ☐ TOBACCO
- ☐ CHOCOLATE
- ☐ EARTH
- ☐ PEPPER
- ☐ VANILLA
- ☐ COFFEE
- ☐ LICORICE
- ☐ LEATHER
- ☐ TOAST
- ☐ GRASS
- ☐ CITRUS
- ☐ MELON
- ☐ LYCHEE
- ☐ ALMOND
- ☐ NUTMEG
- ☐ VEGETAL
- ☐ FLORAL
- ☐ HONEY
- ☐ PEARS
- ☐ PEACHES
- ☐ ....
- ☐ ....
- ☐ ....
- ☐ ....
- ☐ ....
- ☐ ....

DRY / SWEETNESS

1	2	3	4	5	6	7	8	9	10

BALANCE

1	2	3	4	5	6	7	8	9	10

TANNINS

1	2	3	4	5	6	7	8	9	10

FLOVOUR INTENSITY

1	2	3	4	5	6	7	8	9	10

FINISH

SHORT	SHORT TO MED.	MEDIUM	MED. TO LONG	LONG

NOTES
_____
_____
_____
_____

PRICE TO VALUE

1	2	3	4	5	6	7	8	9	10

OVERALL RATING

1	2	3	4	5	6	7	8	9	10

WINE		DATE	
GRAPE		VINTAGE	
PRODUCER		REGION	
PRICE		ALCHOOL %	

COLOR

RED	WHITE	ROSE'	SPARKLING	EFFERVESCENT	FORTIFIED

APPEARANCE

THIN	TRANSLUCENT	SATURATED	OPAQUE

BODY

LIGHT	LIGHT TO MED.	MEDIUM	MED. TO FULL	FULL

SMELL

☐ TOAST	☐ COFFEE	☐ CITRUS	☐ HONEY	☐ ....
☐ TOBACCO	☐ SMOKE	☐ MELON	☐ APPLE	☐ ....
☐ LEATHER	☐ PEPPER	☐ OAK	☐ TROPICAL	☐ ....
☐ MUSHROOM	☐ MINT	☐ BERRIES	☐ GRASS	☐ ....
☐ JAM	☐ SPICE	☐ NUTMEG	☐ FLORAL	☐ ....
☐ CHOCOLATE	☐ ALMOND	☐ VEGETAL	☐ BUTTER	☐ ....

TASTE

☐ DARK FRUIT	☐ EARTH	☐ TOAST	☐ NUTMEG	☐ ....
☐ BERRIES	☐ PEPPER	☐ GRASS	☐ VEGETAL	☐ ....
☐ PLUMS	☐ VANILLA	☐ CITRUS	☐ FLORAL	☐ ....
☐ MUSHROOM	☐ COFFEE	☐ MELON	☐ HONEY	☐ ....
☐ TOBACCO	☐ LICORICE	☐ LYCHEE	☐ PEARS	☐ ....
☐ CHOCOLATE	☐ LEATHER	☐ ALMOND	☐ PEACHES	☐ ....

DRY / SWEETNESS
1	2	3	4	5	6	7	8	9	10

BALANCE
1	2	3	4	5	6	7	8	9	10

TANNINS
1	2	3	4	5	6	7	8	9	10

FLOVOUR INTENSITY
1	2	3	4	5	6	7	8	9	10

FINISH

SHORT	SHORT TO MED.	MEDIUM	MED. TO LONG	LONG

NOTES

PRICE TO VALUE
1	2	3	4	5	6	7	8	9	10

OVERALL RATING
1	2	3	4	5	6	7	8	9	10

WINE _____   **DATE** _____

GRAPE _____   **VINTAGE** _____
PRODUCER _____   **REGION** _____
PRICE _____   **ALCHOOL %** _____

COLOR

RED	WHITE	ROSE'	SPARKLING	EFFERVESCENT	FORTIFIED

APPEARANCE

THIN	TRANSLUCENT	SATURATED	OPAQUE

BODY

LIGHT	LIGHT TO MED.	MEDIUM	MED. TO FULL	FULL

SMELL

- ☐ TOAST
- ☐ TOBACCO
- ☐ LEATHER
- ☐ MUSHROOM
- ☐ JAM
- ☐ CHOCOLATE
- ☐ COFFEE
- ☐ SMOKE
- ☐ PEPPER
- ☐ MINT
- ☐ SPICE
- ☐ ALMOND
- ☐ CITRUS
- ☐ MELON
- ☐ OAK
- ☐ BERRIES
- ☐ NUTMEG
- ☐ VEGETAL
- ☐ HONEY
- ☐ APPLE
- ☐ TROPICAL
- ☐ GRASS
- ☐ FLORAL
- ☐ BUTTER
- ☐ ....
- ☐ ....
- ☐ ....
- ☐ ....
- ☐ ....
- ☐ ....

TASTE

- ☐ DARK FRUIT
- ☐ BERRIES
- ☐ PLUMS
- ☐ MUSHROOM
- ☐ TOBACCO
- ☐ CHOCOLATE
- ☐ EARTH
- ☐ PEPPER
- ☐ VANILLA
- ☐ COFFEE
- ☐ LICORICE
- ☐ LEATHER
- ☐ TOAST
- ☐ GRASS
- ☐ CITRUS
- ☐ MELON
- ☐ LYCHEE
- ☐ ALMOND
- ☐ NUTMEG
- ☐ VEGETAL
- ☐ FLORAL
- ☐ HONEY
- ☐ PEARS
- ☐ PEACHES
- ☐ ....
- ☐ ....
- ☐ ....
- ☐ ....
- ☐ ....
- ☐ ....

DRY / SWEETNESS

1	2	3	4	5	6	7	8	9	10

BALANCE

1	2	3	4	5	6	7	8	9	10

TANNINS

1	2	3	4	5	6	7	8	9	10

FLOVOUR INTENSITY

1	2	3	4	5	6	7	8	9	10

FINISH

SHORT	SHORT TO MED.	MEDIUM	MED. TO LONG	LONG

NOTES

PRICE TO VALUE

1	2	3	4	5	6	7	8	9	10

OVERALL RATING

1	2	3	4	5	6	7	8	9	10

WINE		DATE	
GRAPE		VINTAGE	
PRODUCER		REGION	
PRICE		ALCHOOL %	

COLOR

RED	WHITE	ROSE'	SPARKLING	EFFERVESCENT	FORTIFIED

APPEARANCE

THIN	TRANSLUCENT	SATURATED	OPAQUE

BODY

LIGHT	LIGHT TO MED.	MEDIUM	MED. TO FULL	FULL

SMELL

- ☐ TOAST
- ☐ TOBACCO
- ☐ LEATHER
- ☐ MUSHROOM
- ☐ JAM
- ☐ CHOCOLATE
- ☐ COFFEE
- ☐ SMOKE
- ☐ PEPPER
- ☐ MINT
- ☐ SPICE
- ☐ ALMOND
- ☐ CITRUS
- ☐ MELON
- ☐ OAK
- ☐ BERRIES
- ☐ NUTMEG
- ☐ VEGETAL
- ☐ HONEY
- ☐ APPLE
- ☐ TROPICAL
- ☐ GRASS
- ☐ FLORAL
- ☐ BUTTER
- ☐ ....
- ☐ ....
- ☐ ....
- ☐ ....
- ☐ ....
- ☐ ....

TASTE

- ☐ DARK FRUIT
- ☐ BERRIES
- ☐ PLUMS
- ☐ MUSHROOM
- ☐ TOBACCO
- ☐ CHOCOLATE
- ☐ EARTH
- ☐ PEPPER
- ☐ VANILLA
- ☐ COFFEE
- ☐ LICORICE
- ☐ LEATHER
- ☐ TOAST
- ☐ GRASS
- ☐ CITRUS
- ☐ MELON
- ☐ LYCHEE
- ☐ ALMOND
- ☐ NUTMEG
- ☐ VEGETAL
- ☐ FLORAL
- ☐ HONEY
- ☐ PEARS
- ☐ PEACHES
- ☐ ....
- ☐ ....
- ☐ ....
- ☐ ....
- ☐ ....
- ☐ ....

DRY / SWEETNESS

1	2	3	4	5	6	7	8	9	10

BALANCE

1	2	3	4	5	6	7	8	9	10

TANNINS

1	2	3	4	5	6	7	8	9	10

FLOVOUR INTENSITY

1	2	3	4	5	6	7	8	9	10

FINISH

SHORT	SHORT TO MED.	MEDIUM	MED. TO LONG	LONG

NOTES

PRICE TO VALUE

1	2	3	4	5	6	7	8	9	10

OVERALL RATING

1	2	3	4	5	6	7	8	9	10

WINE		DATE	
GRAPE		VINTAGE	
PRODUCER		REGION	
PRICE		ALCHOOL %	

COLOR

RED	WHITE	ROSE	SPARKLING	EFFERVESCENT	FORTIFIED

APPEARANCE

THIN	TRANSLUCENT	SATURATED	OPAQUE

BODY

LIGHT	LIGHT TO MED.	MEDIUM	MED. TO FULL	FULL

SMELL

- ☐ TOAST
- ☐ TOBACCO
- ☐ LEATHER
- ☐ MUSHROOM
- ☐ JAM
- ☐ CHOCOLATE
- ☐ COFFEE
- ☐ SMOKE
- ☐ PEPPER
- ☐ MINT
- ☐ SPICE
- ☐ ALMOND
- ☐ CITRUS
- ☐ MELON
- ☐ OAK
- ☐ BERRIES
- ☐ NUTMEG
- ☐ VEGETAL
- ☐ HONEY
- ☐ APPLE
- ☐ TROPICAL
- ☐ GRASS
- ☐ FLORAL
- ☐ BUTTER
- ☐ ....
- ☐ ....
- ☐ ....
- ☐ ....
- ☐ ....
- ☐ ....

TASTE

- ☐ DARK FRUIT
- ☐ BERRIES
- ☐ PLUMS
- ☐ MUSHROOM
- ☐ TOBACCO
- ☐ CHOCOLATE
- ☐ EARTH
- ☐ PEPPER
- ☐ VANILLA
- ☐ COFFEE
- ☐ LICORICE
- ☐ LEATHER
- ☐ TOAST
- ☐ GRASS
- ☐ CITRUS
- ☐ MELON
- ☐ LYCHEE
- ☐ ALMOND
- ☐ NUTMEG
- ☐ VEGETAL
- ☐ FLORAL
- ☐ HONEY
- ☐ PEARS
- ☐ PEACHES
- ☐ ....
- ☐ ....
- ☐ ....
- ☐ ....
- ☐ ....
- ☐ ....

DRY / SWEETNESS

1	2	3	4	5	6	7	8	9	10

BALANCE

1	2	3	4	5	6	7	8	9	10

TANNINS

1	2	3	4	5	6	7	8	9	10

FLOVOUR INTENSITY

1	2	3	4	5	6	7	8	9	10

FINISH

SHORT	SHORT TO MED.	MEDIUM	MED. TO LONG	LONG

NOTES

PRICE TO VALUE

1	2	3	4	5	6	7	8	9	10

OVERALL RATING

1	2	3	4	5	6	7	8	9	10

WINE		DATE	
GRAPE		VINTAGE	
PRODUCER		REGION	
PRICE		ALCHOOL %	

COLOR

RED	WHITE	ROSE	SPARKLING	EFFERVESCENT	FORTIFIED

APPEARANCE

THIN	TRANSLUCENT	SATURATED	OPAQUE

BODY

LIGHT	LIGHT TO MED.	MEDIUM	MED. TO FULL	FULL

SMELL

- ☐ TOAST
- ☐ TOBACCO
- ☐ LEATHER
- ☐ MUSHROOM
- ☐ JAM
- ☐ CHOCOLATE
- ☐ COFFEE
- ☐ SMOKE
- ☐ PEPPER
- ☐ MINT
- ☐ SPICE
- ☐ ALMOND
- ☐ CITRUS
- ☐ MELON
- ☐ OAK
- ☐ BERRIES
- ☐ NUTMEG
- ☐ VEGETAL
- ☐ HONEY
- ☐ APPLE
- ☐ TROPICAL
- ☐ GRASS
- ☐ FLORAL
- ☐ BUTTER
- ☐ ....
- ☐ ....
- ☐ ....
- ☐ ....
- ☐ ....
- ☐ ....

TASTE

- ☐ DARK FRUIT
- ☐ BERRIES
- ☐ PLUMS
- ☐ MUSHROOM
- ☐ TOBACCO
- ☐ CHOCOLATE
- ☐ EARTH
- ☐ PEPPER
- ☐ VANILLA
- ☐ COFFEE
- ☐ LICORICE
- ☐ LEATHER
- ☐ TOAST
- ☐ GRASS
- ☐ CITRUS
- ☐ MELON
- ☐ LYCHEE
- ☐ ALMOND
- ☐ NUTMEG
- ☐ VEGETAL
- ☐ FLORAL
- ☐ HONEY
- ☐ PEARS
- ☐ PEACHES
- ☐ ....
- ☐ ....
- ☐ ....
- ☐ ....
- ☐ ....
- ☐ ....

DRY / SWEETNESS
1	2	3	4	5	6	7	8	9	10

BALANCE
1	2	3	4	5	6	7	8	9	10

TANNINS
1	2	3	4	5	6	7	8	9	10

FLOVOUR INTENSITY
1	2	3	4	5	6	7	8	9	10

FINISH

SHORT	SHORT TO MED.	MEDIUM	MED. TO LONG	LONG

NOTES

PRICE TO VALUE
1	2	3	4	5	6	7	8	9	10

OVERALL RATING
1	2	3	4	5	6	7	8	9	10

WINE _____ **DATE** _____

GRAPE _____ **VINTAGE** _____
PRODUCER _____ **REGION** _____
PRICE _____ **ALCHOOL %** _____

COLOR

| RED | WHITE | ROSE' | SPARKLING | EFFERVESCENT | FORTIFIED |

APPEARANCE

| THIN | TRANSLUCENT | SATURATED | OPAQUE |

BODY

| LIGHT | LIGHT TO MED. | MEDIUM | MED. TO FULL | FULL |

SMELL

☐ TOAST	☐ COFFEE	☐ CITRUS	☐ HONEY	☐ ....
☐ TOBACCO	☐ SMOKE	☐ MELON	☐ APPLE	☐ ....
☐ LEATHER	☐ PEPPER	☐ OAK	☐ TROPICAL	☐ ....
☐ MUSHROOM	☐ MINT	☐ BERRIES	☐ GRASS	☐ ....
☐ JAM	☐ SPICE	☐ NUTMEG	☐ FLORAL	☐ ....
☐ CHOCOLATE	☐ ALMOND	☐ VEGETAL	☐ BUTTER	☐ ....

TASTE

☐ DARK FRUIT	☐ EARTH	☐ TOAST	☐ NUTMEG	☐ ....
☐ BERRIES	☐ PEPPER	☐ GRASS	☐ VEGETAL	☐ ....
☐ PLUMS	☐ VANILLA	☐ CITRUS	☐ FLORAL	☐ ....
☐ MUSHROOM	☐ COFFEE	☐ MELON	☐ HONEY	☐ ....
☐ TOBACCO	☐ LICORICE	☐ LYCHEE	☐ PEARS	☐ ....
☐ CHOCOLATE	☐ LEATHER	☐ ALMOND	☐ PEACHES	☐ ....

DRY / SWEETNESS   **BALANCE**
| 1 | 2 | 3 | 4 | 5 | 6 | 7 | 8 | 9 | 10 | | 1 | 2 | 3 | 4 | 5 | 6 | 7 | 8 | 9 | 10 |

TANNINS   **FLOVOUR INTENSITY**
| 1 | 2 | 3 | 4 | 5 | 6 | 7 | 8 | 9 | 10 | | 1 | 2 | 3 | 4 | 5 | 6 | 7 | 8 | 9 | 10 |

FINISH

| SHORT | SHORT TO MED. | MEDIUM | MED. TO LONG | LONG |

NOTES
_____
_____
_____
_____

PRICE TO VALUE   **OVERALL RATING**
| 1 | 2 | 3 | 4 | 5 | 6 | 7 | 8 | 9 | 10 | | 1 | 2 | 3 | 4 | 5 | 6 | 7 | 8 | 9 | 10 |

WINE _____   **DATE** _____

GRAPE _____   **VINTAGE** _____
PRODUCER _____   **REGION** _____
PRICE _____   **ALCHOOL %** _____

COLOR

| RED | WHITE | ROSE' | SPARKLING | EFFERVESCENT | FORTIFIED |

APPEARANCE

| THIN | TRANSLUCENT | SATURATED | OPAQUE |

BODY

| LIGHT | LIGHT TO MED. | MEDIUM | MED. TO FULL | FULL |

SMELL

- ☐ TOAST
- ☐ TOBACCO
- ☐ LEATHER
- ☐ MUSHROOM
- ☐ JAM
- ☐ CHOCOLATE
- ☐ COFFEE
- ☐ SMOKE
- ☐ PEPPER
- ☐ MINT
- ☐ SPICE
- ☐ ALMOND
- ☐ CITRUS
- ☐ MELON
- ☐ OAK
- ☐ BERRIES
- ☐ NUTMEG
- ☐ VEGETAL
- ☐ HONEY
- ☐ APPLE
- ☐ TROPICAL
- ☐ GRASS
- ☐ FLORAL
- ☐ BUTTER
- ☐ ....
- ☐ ....
- ☐ ....
- ☐ ....
- ☐ ....
- ☐ ....

TASTE

- ☐ DARK FRUIT
- ☐ BERRIES
- ☐ PLUMS
- ☐ MUSHROOM
- ☐ TOBACCO
- ☐ CHOCOLATE
- ☐ EARTH
- ☐ PEPPER
- ☐ VANILLA
- ☐ COFFEE
- ☐ LICORICE
- ☐ LEATHER
- ☐ TOAST
- ☐ GRASS
- ☐ CITRUS
- ☐ MELON
- ☐ LYCHEE
- ☐ ALMOND
- ☐ NUTMEG
- ☐ VEGETAL
- ☐ FLORAL
- ☐ HONEY
- ☐ PEARS
- ☐ PEACHES
- ☐ ....
- ☐ ....
- ☐ ....
- ☐ ....
- ☐ ....
- ☐ ....

DRY / SWEETNESS
| 1 | 2 | 3 | 4 | 5 | 6 | 7 | 8 | 9 | 10 |

BALANCE
| 1 | 2 | 3 | 4 | 5 | 6 | 7 | 8 | 9 | 10 |

TANNINS
| 1 | 2 | 3 | 4 | 5 | 6 | 7 | 8 | 9 | 10 |

FLOVOUR INTENSITY
| 1 | 2 | 3 | 4 | 5 | 6 | 7 | 8 | 9 | 10 |

FINISH

| SHORT | SHORT TO MED. | MEDIUM | MED. TO LONG | LONG |

NOTES

_____
_____
_____
_____
_____

PRICE TO VALUE
| 1 | 2 | 3 | 4 | 5 | 6 | 7 | 8 | 9 | 10 |

OVERALL RATING
| 1 | 2 | 3 | 4 | 5 | 6 | 7 | 8 | 9 | 10 |

WINE _____ **DATE** _____

GRAPE _____ **VINTAGE** _____
PRODUCER _____ **REGION** _____
PRICE _____ **ALCHOOL %** _____

COLOR

RED	WHITE	ROSE'	SPARKLING	EFFERVESCENT	FORTIFIED

APPEARANCE

THIN	TRANSLUCENT	SATURATED	OPAQUE

BODY

LIGHT	LIGHT TO MED.	MEDIUM	MED. TO FULL	FULL

SMELL

- ☐ TOAST
- ☐ TOBACCO
- ☐ LEATHER
- ☐ MUSHROOM
- ☐ JAM
- ☐ CHOCOLATE
- ☐ COFFEE
- ☐ SMOKE
- ☐ PEPPER
- ☐ MINT
- ☐ SPICE
- ☐ ALMOND
- ☐ CITRUS
- ☐ MELON
- ☐ OAK
- ☐ BERRIES
- ☐ NUTMEG
- ☐ VEGETAL
- ☐ HONEY
- ☐ APPLE
- ☐ TROPICAL
- ☐ GRASS
- ☐ FLORAL
- ☐ BUTTER
- ☐ ....
- ☐ ....
- ☐ ....
- ☐ ....
- ☐ ....
- ☐ ....

TASTE

- ☐ DARK FRUIT
- ☐ BERRIES
- ☐ PLUMS
- ☐ MUSHROOM
- ☐ TOBACCO
- ☐ CHOCOLATE
- ☐ EARTH
- ☐ PEPPER
- ☐ VANILLA
- ☐ COFFEE
- ☐ LICORICE
- ☐ LEATHER
- ☐ TOAST
- ☐ GRASS
- ☐ CITRUS
- ☐ MELON
- ☐ LYCHEE
- ☐ ALMOND
- ☐ NUTMEG
- ☐ VEGETAL
- ☐ FLORAL
- ☐ HONEY
- ☐ PEARS
- ☐ PEACHES
- ☐ ....
- ☐ ....
- ☐ ....
- ☐ ....
- ☐ ....
- ☐ ....

DRY / SWEETNESS
1	2	3	4	5	6	7	8	9	10

BALANCE
1	2	3	4	5	6	7	8	9	10

TANNINS
1	2	3	4	5	6	7	8	9	10

FLOVOUR INTENSITY
1	2	3	4	5	6	7	8	9	10

FINISH

SHORT	SHORT TO MED.	MEDIUM	MED. TO LONG	LONG

NOTES

_____
_____
_____
_____
_____

PRICE TO VALUE
1	2	3	4	5	6	7	8	9	10

OVERALL RATING
1	2	3	4	5	6	7	8	9	10

WINE _____ **DATE** _____

GRAPE _____ **VINTAGE** _____
PRODUCER _____ **REGION** _____
PRICE _____ **ALCHOOL %** _____

COLOR

RED	WHITE	ROSE'	SPARKLING	EFFERVESCENT	FORTIFIED

APPEARANCE

THIN	TRANSLUCENT	SATURATED	OPAQUE

BODY

LIGHT	LIGHT TO MED.	MEDIUM	MED. TO FULL	FULL

SMELL

- ☐ TOAST
- ☐ TOBACCO
- ☐ LEATHER
- ☐ MUSHROOM
- ☐ JAM
- ☐ CHOCOLATE
- ☐ COFFEE
- ☐ SMOKE
- ☐ PEPPER
- ☐ MINT
- ☐ SPICE
- ☐ ALMOND
- ☐ CITRUS
- ☐ MELON
- ☐ OAK
- ☐ BERRIES
- ☐ NUTMEG
- ☐ VEGETAL
- ☐ HONEY
- ☐ APPLE
- ☐ TROPICAL
- ☐ GRASS
- ☐ FLORAL
- ☐ BUTTER
- ☐ ....
- ☐ ....
- ☐ ....
- ☐ ....
- ☐ ....
- ☐ ....

TASTE

- ☐ DARK FRUIT
- ☐ BERRIES
- ☐ PLUMS
- ☐ MUSHROOM
- ☐ TOBACCO
- ☐ CHOCOLATE
- ☐ EARTH
- ☐ PEPPER
- ☐ VANILLA
- ☐ COFFEE
- ☐ LICORICE
- ☐ LEATHER
- ☐ TOAST
- ☐ GRASS
- ☐ CITRUS
- ☐ MELON
- ☐ LYCHEE
- ☐ ALMOND
- ☐ NUTMEG
- ☐ VEGETAL
- ☐ FLORAL
- ☐ HONEY
- ☐ PEARS
- ☐ PEACHES
- ☐ ....
- ☐ ....
- ☐ ....
- ☐ ....
- ☐ ....
- ☐ ....

DRY / SWEETNESS
1	2	3	4	5	6	7	8	9	10

BALANCE
1	2	3	4	5	6	7	8	9	10

TANNINS
1	2	3	4	5	6	7	8	9	10

FLOVOUR INTENSITY
1	2	3	4	5	6	7	8	9	10

FINISH

SHORT	SHORT TO MED.	MEDIUM	MED. TO LONG	LONG

NOTES

PRICE TO VALUE
1	2	3	4	5	6	7	8	9	10

OVERALL RATING
1	2	3	4	5	6	7	8	9	10

WINE _____   **DATE** _____

GRAPE _____   **VINTAGE** _____
PRODUCER _____   **REGION** _____
PRICE _____   **ALCHOOL %** _____

COLOR
| RED | WHITE | ROSE | SPARKLING | EFFERVESCENT | FORTIFIED |

APPEARANCE
| THIN | TRANSLUCENT | SATURATED | OPAQUE |

BODY
| LIGHT | LIGHT TO MED. | MEDIUM | MED. TO FULL | FULL |

SMELL
- ☐ TOAST
- ☐ TOBACCO
- ☐ LEATHER
- ☐ MUSHROOM
- ☐ JAM
- ☐ CHOCOLATE
- ☐ COFFEE
- ☐ SMOKE
- ☐ PEPPER
- ☐ MINT
- ☐ SPICE
- ☐ ALMOND
- ☐ CITRUS
- ☐ MELON
- ☐ OAK
- ☐ BERRIES
- ☐ NUTMEG
- ☐ VEGETAL
- ☐ HONEY
- ☐ APPLE
- ☐ TROPICAL
- ☐ GRASS
- ☐ FLORAL
- ☐ BUTTER
- ☐ ....
- ☐ ....
- ☐ ....
- ☐ ....
- ☐ ....
- ☐ ....

TASTE
- ☐ DARK FRUIT
- ☐ BERRIES
- ☐ PLUMS
- ☐ MUSHROOM
- ☐ TOBACCO
- ☐ CHOCOLATE
- ☐ EARTH
- ☐ PEPPER
- ☐ VANILLA
- ☐ COFFEE
- ☐ LICORICE
- ☐ LEATHER
- ☐ TOAST
- ☐ GRASS
- ☐ CITRUS
- ☐ MELON
- ☐ LYCHEE
- ☐ ALMOND
- ☐ NUTMEG
- ☐ VEGETAL
- ☐ FLORAL
- ☐ HONEY
- ☐ PEARS
- ☐ PEACHES
- ☐ ....
- ☐ ....
- ☐ ....
- ☐ ....
- ☐ ....
- ☐ ....

DRY / SWEETNESS
| 1 | 2 | 3 | 4 | 5 | 6 | 7 | 8 | 9 | 10 |

BALANCE
| 1 | 2 | 3 | 4 | 5 | 6 | 7 | 8 | 9 | 10 |

TANNINS
| 1 | 2 | 3 | 4 | 5 | 6 | 7 | 8 | 9 | 10 |

FLOVOUR INTENSITY
| 1 | 2 | 3 | 4 | 5 | 6 | 7 | 8 | 9 | 10 |

FINISH
| SHORT | SHORT TO MED. | MEDIUM | MED. TO LONG | LONG |

NOTES
_____
_____
_____
_____
_____

PRICE TO VALUE
| 1 | 2 | 3 | 4 | 5 | 6 | 7 | 8 | 9 | 10 |

OVERALL RATING
| 1 | 2 | 3 | 4 | 5 | 6 | 7 | 8 | 9 | 10 |

WINE _____ **DATE** _____

GRAPE _____ **VINTAGE** _____
PRODUCER _____ **REGION** _____
PRICE _____ **ALCHOOL %** _____

COLOR

RED	WHITE	ROSE	SPARKLING	EFFERVESCENT	FORTIFIED

APPEARANCE

THIN	TRANSLUCENT	SATURATED	OPAQUE

BODY

LIGHT	LIGHT TO MED.	MEDIUM	MED. TO FULL	FULL

SMELL

- ☐ TOAST
- ☐ TOBACCO
- ☐ LEATHER
- ☐ MUSHROOM
- ☐ JAM
- ☐ CHOCOLATE
- ☐ COFFEE
- ☐ SMOKE
- ☐ PEPPER
- ☐ MINT
- ☐ SPICE
- ☐ ALMOND
- ☐ CITRUS
- ☐ MELON
- ☐ OAK
- ☐ BERRIES
- ☐ NUTMEG
- ☐ VEGETAL
- ☐ HONEY
- ☐ APPLE
- ☐ TROPICAL
- ☐ GRASS
- ☐ FLORAL
- ☐ BUTTER
- ☐ ....
- ☐ ....
- ☐ ....
- ☐ ....
- ☐ ....
- ☐ ....

TASTE

- ☐ DARK FRUIT
- ☐ BERRIES
- ☐ PLUMS
- ☐ MUSHROOM
- ☐ TOBACCO
- ☐ CHOCOLATE
- ☐ EARTH
- ☐ PEPPER
- ☐ VANILLA
- ☐ COFFEE
- ☐ LICORICE
- ☐ LEATHER
- ☐ TOAST
- ☐ GRASS
- ☐ CITRUS
- ☐ MELON
- ☐ LYCHEE
- ☐ ALMOND
- ☐ NUTMEG
- ☐ VEGETAL
- ☐ FLORAL
- ☐ HONEY
- ☐ PEARS
- ☐ PEACHES
- ☐ ....
- ☐ ....
- ☐ ....
- ☐ ....
- ☐ ....
- ☐ ....

DRY / SWEETNESS
1	2	3	4	5	6	7	8	9	10

BALANCE
1	2	3	4	5	6	7	8	9	10

TANNINS
1	2	3	4	5	6	7	8	9	10

FLOVOUR INTENSITY
1	2	3	4	5	6	7	8	9	10

FINISH

SHORT	SHORT TO MED.	MEDIUM	MED. TO LONG	LONG

NOTES

_____
_____
_____
_____
_____

PRICE TO VALUE
1	2	3	4	5	6	7	8	9	10

OVERALL RATING
1	2	3	4	5	6	7	8	9	10

WINE _____ **DATE** _____

GRAPE _____ **VINTAGE** _____
PRODUCER _____ **REGION** _____
PRICE _____ **ALCHOOL %** _____

COLOR

RED	WHITE	ROSE	SPARKLING	EFFERVESCENT	FORTIFIED

APPEARANCE

THIN	TRANSLUCENT	SATURATED	OPAQUE

BODY

LIGHT	LIGHT TO MED.	MEDIUM	MED. TO FULL	FULL

SMELL

☐ TOAST	☐ COFFEE	☐ CITRUS	☐ HONEY	☐ ....
☐ TOBACCO	☐ SMOKE	☐ MELON	☐ APPLE	☐ ....
☐ LEATHER	☐ PEPPER	☐ OAK	☐ TROPICAL	☐ ....
☐ MUSHROOM	☐ MINT	☐ BERRIES	☐ GRASS	☐ ....
☐ JAM	☐ SPICE	☐ NUTMEG	☐ FLORAL	☐ ....
☐ CHOCOLATE	☐ ALMOND	☐ VEGETAL	☐ BUTTER	☐ ....

TASTE

☐ DARK FRUIT	☐ EARTH	☐ TOAST	☐ NUTMEG	☐ ....
☐ BERRIES	☐ PEPPER	☐ GRASS	☐ VEGETAL	☐ ....
☐ PLUMS	☐ VANILLA	☐ CITRUS	☐ FLORAL	☐ ....
☐ MUSHROOM	☐ COFFEE	☐ MELON	☐ HONEY	☐ ....
☐ TOBACCO	☐ LICORICE	☐ LYCHEE	☐ PEARS	☐ ....
☐ CHOCOLATE	☐ LEATHER	☐ ALMOND	☐ PEACHES	☐ ....

DRY / SWEETNESS
1	2	3	4	5	6	7	8	9	10

BALANCE
1	2	3	4	5	6	7	8	9	10

TANNINS
1	2	3	4	5	6	7	8	9	10

FLOVOUR INTENSITY
1	2	3	4	5	6	7	8	9	10

FINISH

SHORT	SHORT TO MED.	MEDIUM	MED. TO LONG	LONG

NOTES

_____
_____
_____
_____
_____

PRICE TO VALUE
1	2	3	4	5	6	7	8	9	10

OVERALL RATING
1	2	3	4	5	6	7	8	9	10

WINE _____ **DATE** _____

GRAPE _____ **VINTAGE** _____
PRODUCER _____ **REGION** _____
PRICE _____ **ALCHOOL %** _____

COLOR
| RED | WHITE | ROSE' | SPARKLING | EFFERVESCENT | FORTIFIED |

APPEARANCE
| THIN | TRANSLUCENT | SATURATED | OPAQUE |

BODY
| LIGHT | LIGHT TO MED. | MEDIUM | MED. TO FULL | FULL |

SMELL
- ☐ TOAST
- ☐ TOBACCO
- ☐ LEATHER
- ☐ MUSHROOM
- ☐ JAM
- ☐ CHOCOLATE
- ☐ COFFEE
- ☐ SMOKE
- ☐ PEPPER
- ☐ MINT
- ☐ SPICE
- ☐ ALMOND
- ☐ CITRUS
- ☐ MELON
- ☐ OAK
- ☐ BERRIES
- ☐ NUTMEG
- ☐ VEGETAL
- ☐ HONEY
- ☐ APPLE
- ☐ TROPICAL
- ☐ GRASS
- ☐ FLORAL
- ☐ BUTTER
- ☐ ....
- ☐ ....
- ☐ ....
- ☐ ....
- ☐ ....
- ☐ ....

TASTE
- ☐ DARK FRUIT
- ☐ BERRIES
- ☐ PLUMS
- ☐ MUSHROOM
- ☐ TOBACCO
- ☐ CHOCOLATE
- ☐ EARTH
- ☐ PEPPER
- ☐ VANILLA
- ☐ COFFEE
- ☐ LICORICE
- ☐ LEATHER
- ☐ TOAST
- ☐ GRASS
- ☐ CITRUS
- ☐ MELON
- ☐ LYCHEE
- ☐ ALMOND
- ☐ NUTMEG
- ☐ VEGETAL
- ☐ FLORAL
- ☐ HONEY
- ☐ PEARS
- ☐ PEACHES
- ☐ ....
- ☐ ....
- ☐ ....
- ☐ ....
- ☐ ....
- ☐ ....

DRY / SWEETNESS
| 1 | 2 | 3 | 4 | 5 | 6 | 7 | 8 | 9 | 10 |

BALANCE
| 1 | 2 | 3 | 4 | 5 | 6 | 7 | 8 | 9 | 10 |

TANNINS
| 1 | 2 | 3 | 4 | 5 | 6 | 7 | 8 | 9 | 10 |

FLOVOUR INTENSITY
| 1 | 2 | 3 | 4 | 5 | 6 | 7 | 8 | 9 | 10 |

FINISH
| SHORT | SHORT TO MED. | MEDIUM | MED. TO LONG | LONG |

NOTES

PRICE TO VALUE
| 1 | 2 | 3 | 4 | 5 | 6 | 7 | 8 | 9 | 10 |

OVERALL RATING
| 1 | 2 | 3 | 4 | 5 | 6 | 7 | 8 | 9 | 10 |

WINE _____ **DATE** _____

GRAPE _____ **VINTAGE** _____
PRODUCER _____ **REGION** _____
PRICE _____ **ALCHOOL %** _____

COLOR

| RED | WHITE | ROSE' | SPARKLING | EFFERVESCENT | FORTIFIED |

APPEARANCE

| THIN | TRANSLUCENT | SATURATED | OPAQUE |

BODY

| LIGHT | LIGHT TO MED. | MEDIUM | MED. TO FULL | FULL |

SMELL

- ☐ TOAST
- ☐ TOBACCO
- ☐ LEATHER
- ☐ MUSHROOM
- ☐ JAM
- ☐ CHOCOLATE
- ☐ COFFEE
- ☐ SMOKE
- ☐ PEPPER
- ☐ MINT
- ☐ SPICE
- ☐ ALMOND
- ☐ CITRUS
- ☐ MELON
- ☐ OAK
- ☐ BERRIES
- ☐ NUTMEG
- ☐ VEGETAL
- ☐ HONEY
- ☐ APPLE
- ☐ TROPICAL
- ☐ GRASS
- ☐ FLORAL
- ☐ BUTTER
- ☐ ....
- ☐ ....
- ☐ ....
- ☐ ....
- ☐ ....
- ☐ ....

TASTE

- ☐ DARK FRUIT
- ☐ BERRIES
- ☐ PLUMS
- ☐ MUSHROOM
- ☐ TOBACCO
- ☐ CHOCOLATE
- ☐ EARTH
- ☐ PEPPER
- ☐ VANILLA
- ☐ COFFEE
- ☐ LICORICE
- ☐ LEATHER
- ☐ TOAST
- ☐ GRASS
- ☐ CITRUS
- ☐ MELON
- ☐ LYCHEE
- ☐ ALMOND
- ☐ NUTMEG
- ☐ VEGETAL
- ☐ FLORAL
- ☐ HONEY
- ☐ PEARS
- ☐ PEACHES
- ☐ ....
- ☐ ....
- ☐ ....
- ☐ ....
- ☐ ....
- ☐ ....

DRY / SWEETNESS
| 1 | 2 | 3 | 4 | 5 | 6 | 7 | 8 | 9 | 10 |

BALANCE
| 1 | 2 | 3 | 4 | 5 | 6 | 7 | 8 | 9 | 10 |

TANNINS
| 1 | 2 | 3 | 4 | 5 | 6 | 7 | 8 | 9 | 10 |

FLOVOUR INTENSITY
| 1 | 2 | 3 | 4 | 5 | 6 | 7 | 8 | 9 | 10 |

FINISH

| SHORT | SHORT TO MED. | MEDIUM | MED. TO LONG | LONG |

NOTES

PRICE TO VALUE
| 1 | 2 | 3 | 4 | 5 | 6 | 7 | 8 | 9 | 10 |

OVERALL RATING
| 1 | 2 | 3 | 4 | 5 | 6 | 7 | 8 | 9 | 10 |

WINE _____   **DATE** _____

GRAPE _____   **VINTAGE** _____
PRODUCER _____   **REGION** _____
PRICE _____   **ALCHOOL %** _____

COLOR

RED	WHITE	ROSE'	SPARKLING	EFFERVESCENT	FORTIFIED

APPEARANCE

THIN	TRANSLUCENT	SATURATED	OPAQUE

BODY

LIGHT	LIGHT TO MED.	MEDIUM	MED. TO FULL	FULL

SMELL

- ☐ TOAST
- ☐ TOBACCO
- ☐ LEATHER
- ☐ MUSHROOM
- ☐ JAM
- ☐ CHOCOLATE
- ☐ COFFEE
- ☐ SMOKE
- ☐ PEPPER
- ☐ MINT
- ☐ SPICE
- ☐ ALMOND
- ☐ CITRUS
- ☐ MELON
- ☐ OAK
- ☐ BERRIES
- ☐ NUTMEG
- ☐ VEGETAL
- ☐ HONEY
- ☐ APPLE
- ☐ TROPICAL
- ☐ GRASS
- ☐ FLORAL
- ☐ BUTTER
- ☐ ....
- ☐ ....
- ☐ ....
- ☐ ....
- ☐ ....
- ☐ ....

TASTE

- ☐ DARK FRUIT
- ☐ BERRIES
- ☐ PLUMS
- ☐ MUSHROOM
- ☐ TOBACCO
- ☐ CHOCOLATE
- ☐ EARTH
- ☐ PEPPER
- ☐ VANILLA
- ☐ COFFEE
- ☐ LICORICE
- ☐ LEATHER
- ☐ TOAST
- ☐ GRASS
- ☐ CITRUS
- ☐ MELON
- ☐ LYCHEE
- ☐ ALMOND
- ☐ NUTMEG
- ☐ VEGETAL
- ☐ FLORAL
- ☐ HONEY
- ☐ PEARS
- ☐ PEACHES
- ☐ ....
- ☐ ....
- ☐ ....
- ☐ ....
- ☐ ....
- ☐ ....

DRY / SWEETNESS

1	2	3	4	5	6	7	8	9	10

BALANCE

1	2	3	4	5	6	7	8	9	10

TANNINS

1	2	3	4	5	6	7	8	9	10

FLOVOUR INTENSITY

1	2	3	4	5	6	7	8	9	10

FINISH

SHORT	SHORT TO MED.	MEDIUM	MED. TO LONG	LONG

NOTES
_____
_____
_____
_____
_____

PRICE TO VALUE

1	2	3	4	5	6	7	8	9	10

OVERALL RATING

1	2	3	4	5	6	7	8	9	10

WINE   **DATE**

GRAPE   **VINTAGE**
PRODUCER   **REGION**
PRICE   **ALCHOOL %**

COLOR

| RED | WHITE | ROSE | SPARKLING | EFFERVESCENT | FORTIFIED |

APPEARANCE

| THIN | TRANSLUCENT | SATURATED | OPAQUE |

BODY

| LIGHT | LIGHT TO MED. | MEDIUM | MED. TO FULL | FULL |

SMELL

- ☐ TOAST
- ☐ TOBACCO
- ☐ LEATHER
- ☐ MUSHROOM
- ☐ JAM
- ☐ CHOCOLATE
- ☐ COFFEE
- ☐ SMOKE
- ☐ PEPPER
- ☐ MINT
- ☐ SPICE
- ☐ ALMOND
- ☐ CITRUS
- ☐ MELON
- ☐ OAK
- ☐ BERRIES
- ☐ NUTMEG
- ☐ VEGETAL
- ☐ HONEY
- ☐ APPLE
- ☐ TROPICAL
- ☐ GRASS
- ☐ FLORAL
- ☐ BUTTER

TASTE

- ☐ DARK FRUIT
- ☐ BERRIES
- ☐ PLUMS
- ☐ MUSHROOM
- ☐ TOBACCO
- ☐ CHOCOLATE
- ☐ EARTH
- ☐ PEPPER
- ☐ VANILLA
- ☐ COFFEE
- ☐ LICORICE
- ☐ LEATHER
- ☐ TOAST
- ☐ GRASS
- ☐ CITRUS
- ☐ MELON
- ☐ LYCHEE
- ☐ ALMOND
- ☐ NUTMEG
- ☐ VEGETAL
- ☐ FLORAL
- ☐ HONEY
- ☐ PEARS
- ☐ PEACHES

DRY / SWEETNESS
| 1 | 2 | 3 | 4 | 5 | 6 | 7 | 8 | 9 | 10 |

BALANCE
| 1 | 2 | 3 | 4 | 5 | 6 | 7 | 8 | 9 | 10 |

TANNINS
| 1 | 2 | 3 | 4 | 5 | 6 | 7 | 8 | 9 | 10 |

FLOVOUR INTENSITY
| 1 | 2 | 3 | 4 | 5 | 6 | 7 | 8 | 9 | 10 |

FINISH
| SHORT | SHORT TO MED. | MEDIUM | MED. TO LONG | LONG |

NOTES

PRICE TO VALUE
| 1 | 2 | 3 | 4 | 5 | 6 | 7 | 8 | 9 | 10 |

OVERALL RATING
| 1 | 2 | 3 | 4 | 5 | 6 | 7 | 8 | 9 | 10 |

WINE _____ **DATE** _____

GRAPE _____ **VINTAGE** _____
PRODUCER _____ **REGION** _____
PRICE _____ **ALCHOOL %** _____

COLOR

RED	WHITE	ROSE	SPARKLING	EFFERVESCENT	FORTIFIED

APPEARANCE

THIN	TRANSLUCENT	SATURATED	OPAQUE

BODY

LIGHT	LIGHT TO MED.	MEDIUM	MED. TO FULL	FULL

SMELL

- ☐ TOAST
- ☐ TOBACCO
- ☐ LEATHER
- ☐ MUSHROOM
- ☐ JAM
- ☐ CHOCOLATE
- ☐ COFFEE
- ☐ SMOKE
- ☐ PEPPER
- ☐ MINT
- ☐ SPICE
- ☐ ALMOND
- ☐ CITRUS
- ☐ MELON
- ☐ OAK
- ☐ BERRIES
- ☐ NUTMEG
- ☐ VEGETAL
- ☐ HONEY
- ☐ APPLE
- ☐ TROPICAL
- ☐ GRASS
- ☐ FLORAL
- ☐ BUTTER
- ☐ ....
- ☐ ....
- ☐ ....
- ☐ ....
- ☐ ....
- ☐ ....

TASTE

- ☐ DARK FRUIT
- ☐ BERRIES
- ☐ PLUMS
- ☐ MUSHROOM
- ☐ TOBACCO
- ☐ CHOCOLATE
- ☐ EARTH
- ☐ PEPPER
- ☐ VANILLA
- ☐ COFFEE
- ☐ LICORICE
- ☐ LEATHER
- ☐ TOAST
- ☐ GRASS
- ☐ CITRUS
- ☐ MELON
- ☐ LYCHEE
- ☐ ALMOND
- ☐ NUTMEG
- ☐ VEGETAL
- ☐ FLORAL
- ☐ HONEY
- ☐ PEARS
- ☐ PEACHES
- ☐ ....
- ☐ ....
- ☐ ....
- ☐ ....
- ☐ ....
- ☐ ....

DRY / SWEETNESS

1	2	3	4	5	6	7	8	9	10

BALANCE

1	2	3	4	5	6	7	8	9	10

TANNINS

1	2	3	4	5	6	7	8	9	10

FLOVOUR INTENSITY

1	2	3	4	5	6	7	8	9	10

FINISH

SHORT	SHORT TO MED.	MEDIUM	MED. TO LONG	LONG

NOTES

_____
_____
_____
_____
_____

PRICE TO VALUE

1	2	3	4	5	6	7	8	9	10

OVERALL RATING

1	2	3	4	5	6	7	8	9	10

WINE _____ **DATE** _____

GRAPE _____ **VINTAGE** _____
PRODUCER _____ **REGION** _____
PRICE _____ **ALCHOOL %** _____

COLOR

| RED | WHITE | ROSE' | SPARKLING | EFFERVESCENT | FORTIFIED |

APPEARANCE

| THIN | TRANSLUCENT | SATURATED | OPAQUE |

BODY

| LIGHT | LIGHT TO MED. | MEDIUM | MED. TO FULL | FULL |

SMELL

☐ TOAST	☐ COFFEE	☐ CITRUS	☐ HONEY	☐ ....
☐ TOBACCO	☐ SMOKE	☐ MELON	☐ APPLE	☐ ....
☐ LEATHER	☐ PEPPER	☐ OAK	☐ TROPICAL	☐ ....
☐ MUSHROOM	☐ MINT	☐ BERRIES	☐ GRASS	☐ ....
☐ JAM	☐ SPICE	☐ NUTMEG	☐ FLORAL	☐ ....
☐ CHOCOLATE	☐ ALMOND	☐ VEGETAL	☐ BUTTER	☐ ....

TASTE

☐ DARK FRUIT	☐ EARTH	☐ TOAST	☐ NUTMEG	☐ ....
☐ BERRIES	☐ PEPPER	☐ GRASS	☐ VEGETAL	☐ ....
☐ PLUMS	☐ VANILLA	☐ CITRUS	☐ FLORAL	☐ ....
☐ MUSHROOM	☐ COFFEE	☐ MELON	☐ HONEY	☐ ....
☐ TOBACCO	☐ LICORICE	☐ LYCHEE	☐ PEARS	☐ ....
☐ CHOCOLATE	☐ LEATHER	☐ ALMOND	☐ PEACHES	☐ ....

DRY / SWEETNESS
| 1 | 2 | 3 | 4 | 5 | 6 | 7 | 8 | 9 | 10 |

BALANCE
| 1 | 2 | 3 | 4 | 5 | 6 | 7 | 8 | 9 | 10 |

TANNINS
| 1 | 2 | 3 | 4 | 5 | 6 | 7 | 8 | 9 | 10 |

FLOVOUR INTENSITY
| 1 | 2 | 3 | 4 | 5 | 6 | 7 | 8 | 9 | 10 |

FINISH

| SHORT | SHORT TO MED. | MEDIUM | MED. TO LONG | LONG |

NOTES

_____
_____
_____
_____

PRICE TO VALUE
| 1 | 2 | 3 | 4 | 5 | 6 | 7 | 8 | 9 | 10 |

OVERALL RATING
| 1 | 2 | 3 | 4 | 5 | 6 | 7 | 8 | 9 | 10 |

WINE _____ **DATE** _____

GRAPE _____ **VINTAGE** _____
PRODUCER _____ **REGION** _____
PRICE _____ **ALCHOOL %** _____

COLOR

RED	WHITE	ROSE'	SPARKLING	EFFERVESCENT	FORTIFIED

APPEARANCE

THIN	TRANSLUCENT	SATURATED	OPAQUE

BODY

LIGHT	LIGHT TO MED.	MEDIUM	MED. TO FULL	FULL

SMELL

- ☐ TOAST
- ☐ TOBACCO
- ☐ LEATHER
- ☐ MUSHROOM
- ☐ JAM
- ☐ CHOCOLATE
- ☐ COFFEE
- ☐ SMOKE
- ☐ PEPPER
- ☐ MINT
- ☐ SPICE
- ☐ ALMOND
- ☐ CITRUS
- ☐ MELON
- ☐ OAK
- ☐ BERRIES
- ☐ NUTMEG
- ☐ VEGETAL
- ☐ HONEY
- ☐ APPLE
- ☐ TROPICAL
- ☐ GRASS
- ☐ FLORAL
- ☐ BUTTER
- ☐ ....
- ☐ ....
- ☐ ....
- ☐ ....
- ☐ ....
- ☐ ....

TASTE

- ☐ DARK FRUIT
- ☐ BERRIES
- ☐ PLUMS
- ☐ MUSHROOM
- ☐ TOBACCO
- ☐ CHOCOLATE
- ☐ EARTH
- ☐ PEPPER
- ☐ VANILLA
- ☐ COFFEE
- ☐ LICORICE
- ☐ LEATHER
- ☐ TOAST
- ☐ GRASS
- ☐ CITRUS
- ☐ MELON
- ☐ LYCHEE
- ☐ ALMOND
- ☐ NUTMEG
- ☐ VEGETAL
- ☐ FLORAL
- ☐ HONEY
- ☐ PEARS
- ☐ PEACHES
- ☐ ....
- ☐ ....
- ☐ ....
- ☐ ....
- ☐ ....
- ☐ ....

DRY / SWEETNESS
1	2	3	4	5	6	7	8	9	10

BALANCE
1	2	3	4	5	6	7	8	9	10

TANNINS
1	2	3	4	5	6	7	8	9	10

FLOVOUR INTENSITY
1	2	3	4	5	6	7	8	9	10

FINISH

SHORT	SHORT TO MED.	MEDIUM	MED. TO LONG	LONG

NOTES

PRICE TO VALUE
1	2	3	4	5	6	7	8	9	10

OVERALL RATING
1	2	3	4	5	6	7	8	9	10

WINE _____ **DATE** _____

GRAPE _____ **VINTAGE** _____
PRODUCER _____ **REGION** _____
PRICE _____ **ALCHOOL %** _____

COLOR

RED	WHITE	ROSE'	SPARKLING	EFFERVESCENT	FORTIFIED

APPEARANCE

THIN	TRANSLUCENT	SATURATED	OPAQUE

BODY

LIGHT	LIGHT TO MED.	MEDIUM	MED. TO FULL	FULL

SMELL

- ☐ TOAST
- ☐ TOBACCO
- ☐ LEATHER
- ☐ MUSHROOM
- ☐ JAM
- ☐ CHOCOLATE
- ☐ COFFEE
- ☐ SMOKE
- ☐ PEPPER
- ☐ MINT
- ☐ SPICE
- ☐ ALMOND
- ☐ CITRUS
- ☐ MELON
- ☐ OAK
- ☐ BERRIES
- ☐ NUTMEG
- ☐ VEGETAL
- ☐ HONEY
- ☐ APPLE
- ☐ TROPICAL
- ☐ GRASS
- ☐ FLORAL
- ☐ BUTTER
- ☐ ....
- ☐ ....
- ☐ ....
- ☐ ....
- ☐ ....
- ☐ ....

TASTE

- ☐ DARK FRUIT
- ☐ BERRIES
- ☐ PLUMS
- ☐ MUSHROOM
- ☐ TOBACCO
- ☐ CHOCOLATE
- ☐ EARTH
- ☐ PEPPER
- ☐ VANILLA
- ☐ COFFEE
- ☐ LICORICE
- ☐ LEATHER
- ☐ TOAST
- ☐ GRASS
- ☐ CITRUS
- ☐ MELON
- ☐ LYCHEE
- ☐ ALMOND
- ☐ NUTMEG
- ☐ VEGETAL
- ☐ FLORAL
- ☐ HONEY
- ☐ PEARS
- ☐ PEACHES
- ☐ ....
- ☐ ....
- ☐ ....
- ☐ ....
- ☐ ....
- ☐ ....

DRY / SWEETNESS

1	2	3	4	5	6	7	8	9	10

BALANCE

1	2	3	4	5	6	7	8	9	10

TANNINS

1	2	3	4	5	6	7	8	9	10

FLOVOUR INTENSITY

1	2	3	4	5	6	7	8	9	10

FINISH

SHORT	SHORT TO MED.	MEDIUM	MED. TO LONG	LONG

NOTES

PRICE TO VALUE

1	2	3	4	5	6	7	8	9	10

OVERALL RATING

1	2	3	4	5	6	7	8	9	10

WINE		DATE	
GRAPE		**VINTAGE**	
PRODUCER		**REGION**	
PRICE		**ALCHOOL %**	

COLOR

RED	WHITE	ROSE'	SPARKLING	EFFERVESCENT	FORTIFIED

APPEARANCE

THIN	TRANSLUCENT	SATURATED	OPAQUE

BODY

LIGHT	LIGHT TO MED.	MEDIUM	MED. TO FULL	FULL

SMELL

- ☐ TOAST
- ☐ TOBACCO
- ☐ LEATHER
- ☐ MUSHROOM
- ☐ JAM
- ☐ CHOCOLATE
- ☐ COFFEE
- ☐ SMOKE
- ☐ PEPPER
- ☐ MINT
- ☐ SPICE
- ☐ ALMOND
- ☐ CITRUS
- ☐ MELON
- ☐ OAK
- ☐ BERRIES
- ☐ NUTMEG
- ☐ VEGETAL
- ☐ HONEY
- ☐ APPLE
- ☐ TROPICAL
- ☐ GRASS
- ☐ FLORAL
- ☐ BUTTER
- ☐ ....
- ☐ ....
- ☐ ....
- ☐ ....
- ☐ ....
- ☐ ....

TASTE

- ☐ DARK FRUIT
- ☐ BERRIES
- ☐ PLUMS
- ☐ MUSHROOM
- ☐ TOBACCO
- ☐ CHOCOLATE
- ☐ EARTH
- ☐ PEPPER
- ☐ VANILLA
- ☐ COFFEE
- ☐ LICORICE
- ☐ LEATHER
- ☐ TOAST
- ☐ GRASS
- ☐ CITRUS
- ☐ MELON
- ☐ LYCHEE
- ☐ ALMOND
- ☐ NUTMEG
- ☐ VEGETAL
- ☐ FLORAL
- ☐ HONEY
- ☐ PEARS
- ☐ PEACHES
- ☐ ....
- ☐ ....
- ☐ ....
- ☐ ....
- ☐ ....
- ☐ ....

DRY / SWEETNESS

1	2	3	4	5	6	7	8	9	10

BALANCE

1	2	3	4	5	6	7	8	9	10

TANNINS

1	2	3	4	5	6	7	8	9	10

FLOVOUR INTENSITY

1	2	3	4	5	6	7	8	9	10

FINISH

SHORT	SHORT TO MED.	MEDIUM	MED. TO LONG	LONG

NOTES

PRICE TO VALUE

1	2	3	4	5	6	7	8	9	10

OVERALL RATING

1	2	3	4	5	6	7	8	9	10

WINE   **DATE**

GRAPE   **VINTAGE**
PRODUCER   **REGION**
PRICE   **ALCHOOL %**

COLOR

RED	WHITE	ROSE	SPARKLING	EFFERVESCENT	FORTIFIED

APPEARANCE

THIN	TRANSLUCENT	SATURATED	OPAQUE

BODY

LIGHT	LIGHT TO MED.	MEDIUM	MED. TO FULL	FULL

SMELL

- ☐ TOAST
- ☐ TOBACCO
- ☐ LEATHER
- ☐ MUSHROOM
- ☐ JAM
- ☐ CHOCOLATE
- ☐ COFFEE
- ☐ SMOKE
- ☐ PEPPER
- ☐ MINT
- ☐ SPICE
- ☐ ALMOND
- ☐ CITRUS
- ☐ MELON
- ☐ OAK
- ☐ BERRIES
- ☐ NUTMEG
- ☐ VEGETAL
- ☐ HONEY
- ☐ APPLE
- ☐ TROPICAL
- ☐ GRASS
- ☐ FLORAL
- ☐ BUTTER
- ☐ ....
- ☐ ....
- ☐ ....
- ☐ ....
- ☐ ....
- ☐ ....

TASTE

- ☐ DARK FRUIT
- ☐ BERRIES
- ☐ PLUMS
- ☐ MUSHROOM
- ☐ TOBACCO
- ☐ CHOCOLATE
- ☐ EARTH
- ☐ PEPPER
- ☐ VANILLA
- ☐ COFFEE
- ☐ LICORICE
- ☐ LEATHER
- ☐ TOAST
- ☐ GRASS
- ☐ CITRUS
- ☐ MELON
- ☐ LYCHEE
- ☐ ALMOND
- ☐ NUTMEG
- ☐ VEGETAL
- ☐ FLORAL
- ☐ HONEY
- ☐ PEARS
- ☐ PEACHES
- ☐ ....
- ☐ ....
- ☐ ....
- ☐ ....
- ☐ ....
- ☐ ....

DRY / SWEETNESS

1	2	3	4	5	6	7	8	9	10

BALANCE

1	2	3	4	5	6	7	8	9	10

TANNINS

1	2	3	4	5	6	7	8	9	10

FLOVOUR INTENSITY

1	2	3	4	5	6	7	8	9	10

FINISH

SHORT	SHORT TO MED.	MEDIUM	MED. TO LONG	LONG

NOTES

PRICE TO VALUE

1	2	3	4	5	6	7	8	9	10

OVERALL RATING

1	2	3	4	5	6	7	8	9	10

WINE		DATE	
GRAPE		VINTAGE	
PRODUCER		REGION	
PRICE		ALCHOOL %	

COLOR

RED	WHITE	ROSE	SPARKLING	EFFERVESCENT	FORTIFIED

APPEARANCE

THIN	TRANSLUCENT	SATURATED	OPAQUE

BODY

LIGHT	LIGHT TO MED.	MEDIUM	MED. TO FULL	FULL

SMELL

- ☐ TOAST
- ☐ TOBACCO
- ☐ LEATHER
- ☐ MUSHROOM
- ☐ JAM
- ☐ CHOCOLATE
- ☐ COFFEE
- ☐ SMOKE
- ☐ PEPPER
- ☐ MINT
- ☐ SPICE
- ☐ ALMOND
- ☐ CITRUS
- ☐ MELON
- ☐ OAK
- ☐ BERRIES
- ☐ NUTMEG
- ☐ VEGETAL
- ☐ HONEY
- ☐ APPLE
- ☐ TROPICAL
- ☐ GRASS
- ☐ FLORAL
- ☐ BUTTER
- ☐ ....
- ☐ ....
- ☐ ....
- ☐ ....
- ☐ ....
- ☐ ....

TASTE

- ☐ DARK FRUIT
- ☐ BERRIES
- ☐ PLUMS
- ☐ MUSHROOM
- ☐ TOBACCO
- ☐ CHOCOLATE
- ☐ EARTH
- ☐ PEPPER
- ☐ VANILLA
- ☐ COFFEE
- ☐ LICORICE
- ☐ LEATHER
- ☐ TOAST
- ☐ GRASS
- ☐ CITRUS
- ☐ MELON
- ☐ LYCHEE
- ☐ ALMOND
- ☐ NUTMEG
- ☐ VEGETAL
- ☐ FLORAL
- ☐ HONEY
- ☐ PEARS
- ☐ PEACHES
- ☐ ....
- ☐ ....
- ☐ ....
- ☐ ....
- ☐ ....
- ☐ ....

DRY / SWEETNESS

1	2	3	4	5	6	7	8	9	10

BALANCE

1	2	3	4	5	6	7	8	9	10

TANNINS

1	2	3	4	5	6	7	8	9	10

FLOVOUR INTENSITY

1	2	3	4	5	6	7	8	9	10

FINISH

SHORT	SHORT TO MED.	MEDIUM	MED. TO LONG	LONG

NOTES

PRICE TO VALUE

1	2	3	4	5	6	7	8	9	10

OVERALL RATING

1	2	3	4	5	6	7	8	9	10

WINE		DATE	
GRAPE		VINTAGE	
PRODUCER		REGION	
PRICE		ALCHOOL %	

COLOR

RED	WHITE	ROSE'	SPARKLING	EFFERVESCENT	FORTIFIED

APPEARANCE

THIN	TRANSLUCENT	SATURATED	OPAQUE

BODY

LIGHT	LIGHT TO MED.	MEDIUM	MED. TO FULL	FULL

SMELL

☐ TOAST	☐ COFFEE	☐ CITRUS	☐ HONEY	☐ ....
☐ TOBACCO	☐ SMOKE	☐ MELON	☐ APPLE	☐ ....
☐ LEATHER	☐ PEPPER	☐ OAK	☐ TROPICAL	☐ ....
☐ MUSHROOM	☐ MINT	☐ BERRIES	☐ GRASS	☐ ....
☐ JAM	☐ SPICE	☐ NUTMEG	☐ FLORAL	☐ ....
☐ CHOCOLATE	☐ ALMOND	☐ VEGETAL	☐ BUTTER	☐ ....

TASTE

☐ DARK FRUIT	☐ EARTH	☐ TOAST	☐ NUTMEG	☐ ....
☐ BERRIES	☐ PEPPER	☐ GRASS	☐ VEGETAL	☐ ....
☐ PLUMS	☐ VANILLA	☐ CITRUS	☐ FLORAL	☐ ....
☐ MUSHROOM	☐ COFFEE	☐ MELON	☐ HONEY	☐ ....
☐ TOBACCO	☐ LICORICE	☐ LYCHEE	☐ PEARS	☐ ....
☐ CHOCOLATE	☐ LEATHER	☐ ALMOND	☐ PEACHES	☐ ....

DRY / SWEETNESS

1	2	3	4	5	6	7	8	9	10

BALANCE

1	2	3	4	5	6	7	8	9	10

TANNINS

1	2	3	4	5	6	7	8	9	10

FLOVOUR INTENSITY

1	2	3	4	5	6	7	8	9	10

FINISH

SHORT	SHORT TO MED.	MEDIUM	MED. TO LONG	LONG

NOTES

PRICE TO VALUE

1	2	3	4	5	6	7	8	9	10

OVERALL RATING

1	2	3	4	5	6	7	8	9	10

WINE   **DATE**

GRAPE   **VINTAGE**
PRODUCER   **REGION**
PRICE   **ALCHOOL %**

COLOR

RED	WHITE	ROSE'	SPARKLING	EFFERVESCENT	FORTIFIED

APPEARANCE

THIN	TRANSLUCENT	SATURATED	OPAQUE

BODY

LIGHT	LIGHT TO MED.	MEDIUM	MED. TO FULL	FULL

SMELL

☐ TOAST	☐ COFFEE	☐ CITRUS	☐ HONEY	☐ ....
☐ TOBACCO	☐ SMOKE	☐ MELON	☐ APPLE	☐ ....
☐ LEATHER	☐ PEPPER	☐ OAK	☐ TROPICAL	☐ ....
☐ MUSHROOM	☐ MINT	☐ BERRIES	☐ GRASS	☐ ....
☐ JAM	☐ SPICE	☐ NUTMEG	☐ FLORAL	☐ ....
☐ CHOCOLATE	☐ ALMOND	☐ VEGETAL	☐ BUTTER	☐ ....

TASTE

☐ DARK FRUIT	☐ EARTH	☐ TOAST	☐ NUTMEG	☐ ....
☐ BERRIES	☐ PEPPER	☐ GRASS	☐ VEGETAL	☐ ....
☐ PLUMS	☐ VANILLA	☐ CITRUS	☐ FLORAL	☐ ....
☐ MUSHROOM	☐ COFFEE	☐ MELON	☐ HONEY	☐ ....
☐ TOBACCO	☐ LICORICE	☐ LYCHEE	☐ PEARS	☐ ....
☐ CHOCOLATE	☐ LEATHER	☐ ALMOND	☐ PEACHES	☐ ....

DRY / SWEETNESS
1	2	3	4	5	6	7	8	9	10

BALANCE
1	2	3	4	5	6	7	8	9	10

TANNINS
1	2	3	4	5	6	7	8	9	10

FLOVOUR INTENSITY
1	2	3	4	5	6	7	8	9	10

FINISH

SHORT	SHORT TO MED.	MEDIUM	MED. TO LONG	LONG

NOTES

PRICE TO VALUE
1	2	3	4	5	6	7	8	9	10

OVERALL RATING
1	2	3	4	5	6	7	8	9	10

WINE		DATE	
GRAPE		VINTAGE	
PRODUCER		REGION	
PRICE		ALCHOOL %	

COLOR

RED	WHITE	ROSE'	SPARKLING	EFFERVESCENT	FORTIFIED

APPEARANCE

THIN	TRANSLUCENT	SATURATED	OPAQUE

BODY

LIGHT	LIGHT TO MED.	MEDIUM	MED. TO FULL	FULL

SMELL

- ☐ TOAST
- ☐ TOBACCO
- ☐ LEATHER
- ☐ MUSHROOM
- ☐ JAM
- ☐ CHOCOLATE
- ☐ COFFEE
- ☐ SMOKE
- ☐ PEPPER
- ☐ MINT
- ☐ SPICE
- ☐ ALMOND
- ☐ CITRUS
- ☐ MELON
- ☐ OAK
- ☐ BERRIES
- ☐ NUTMEG
- ☐ VEGETAL
- ☐ HONEY
- ☐ APPLE
- ☐ TROPICAL
- ☐ GRASS
- ☐ FLORAL
- ☐ BUTTER
- ☐ ....
- ☐ ....
- ☐ ....
- ☐ ....
- ☐ ....
- ☐ ....

TASTE

- ☐ DARK FRUIT
- ☐ BERRIES
- ☐ PLUMS
- ☐ MUSHROOM
- ☐ TOBACCO
- ☐ CHOCOLATE
- ☐ EARTH
- ☐ PEPPER
- ☐ VANILLA
- ☐ COFFEE
- ☐ LICORICE
- ☐ LEATHER
- ☐ TOAST
- ☐ GRASS
- ☐ CITRUS
- ☐ MELON
- ☐ LYCHEE
- ☐ ALMOND
- ☐ NUTMEG
- ☐ VEGETAL
- ☐ FLORAL
- ☐ HONEY
- ☐ PEARS
- ☐ PEACHES
- ☐ ....
- ☐ ....
- ☐ ....
- ☐ ....
- ☐ ....
- ☐ ....

DRY / SWEETNESS
1	2	3	4	5	6	7	8	9	10

BALANCE
1	2	3	4	5	6	7	8	9	10

TANNINS
1	2	3	4	5	6	7	8	9	10

FLOVOUR INTENSITY
1	2	3	4	5	6	7	8	9	10

FINISH

SHORT	SHORT TO MED.	MEDIUM	MED. TO LONG	LONG

NOTES

PRICE TO VALUE
1	2	3	4	5	6	7	8	9	10

OVERALL RATING
1	2	3	4	5	6	7	8	9	10

WINE		DATE	
GRAPE		VINTAGE	
PRODUCER		REGION	
PRICE		ALCHOOL %	

COLOR

RED	WHITE	ROSE'	SPARKLING	EFFERVESCENT	FORTIFIED

APPEARANCE

THIN	TRANSLUCENT	SATURATED	OPAQUE

BODY

LIGHT	LIGHT TO MED.	MEDIUM	MED. TO FULL	FULL

SMELL

- ☐ TOAST
- ☐ TOBACCO
- ☐ LEATHER
- ☐ MUSHROOM
- ☐ JAM
- ☐ CHOCOLATE
- ☐ COFFEE
- ☐ SMOKE
- ☐ PEPPER
- ☐ MINT
- ☐ SPICE
- ☐ ALMOND
- ☐ CITRUS
- ☐ MELON
- ☐ OAK
- ☐ BERRIES
- ☐ NUTMEG
- ☐ VEGETAL
- ☐ HONEY
- ☐ APPLE
- ☐ TROPICAL
- ☐ GRASS
- ☐ FLORAL
- ☐ BUTTER
- ☐ ....
- ☐ ....
- ☐ ....
- ☐ ....
- ☐ ....
- ☐ ....

TASTE

- ☐ DARK FRUIT
- ☐ BERRIES
- ☐ PLUMS
- ☐ MUSHROOM
- ☐ TOBACCO
- ☐ CHOCOLATE
- ☐ EARTH
- ☐ PEPPER
- ☐ VANILLA
- ☐ COFFEE
- ☐ LICORICE
- ☐ LEATHER
- ☐ TOAST
- ☐ GRASS
- ☐ CITRUS
- ☐ MELON
- ☐ LYCHEE
- ☐ ALMOND
- ☐ NUTMEG
- ☐ VEGETAL
- ☐ FLORAL
- ☐ HONEY
- ☐ PEARS
- ☐ PEACHES
- ☐ ....
- ☐ ....
- ☐ ....
- ☐ ....
- ☐ ....
- ☐ ....

DRY / SWEETNESS

1	2	3	4	5	6	7	8	9	10

BALANCE

1	2	3	4	5	6	7	8	9	10

TANNINS

1	2	3	4	5	6	7	8	9	10

FLOVOUR INTENSITY

1	2	3	4	5	6	7	8	9	10

FINISH

SHORT	SHORT TO MED.	MEDIUM	MED. TO LONG	LONG

NOTES

PRICE TO VALUE

1	2	3	4	5	6	7	8	9	10

OVERALL RATING

1	2	3	4	5	6	7	8	9	10

PERFECT BOUND

Published by Perfect Bound Design and Writing © 2021 Perfect Bound

All rights reserved. No part of this book may be reproduced or trasmitted in any form or by any means, including but not limited to informations storage and retrieval system, electronic, mechanical, photocopy, recording, etc. without written permission from the copyright holder.

CPSIA information can be obtained
at www.ICGtesting.com
Printed in the USA
LVHW052254291121
704802LV00033B/3190